Jeff Gordon

Jeff Gordon

Racing Back to the Front— My Memoir

JEFF GORDON

WITH STEVE EUBANKS

ATRIA BOOKS

NEW YORK   LONDON   TORONTO   SYDNEY   SINGAPORE

ATRIA BOOKS
1230 Avenue of the Americas
New York, NY 10020

Library of Congress Cataloging-in-Publication Data

Gordon, Jeff, 1971–
Jeff Gordon / by Jeff Gordon with Steve Eubanks.—
1st Atria Books hardcover ed.
p. cm.
ISBN 0-7434-6415-X
1. Gordon, Jeff, 1971–
2. Automobile racing drivers—United States—Biography.
I. Eubanks, Steve, 1962–   II. Title.

GV1032.G67G67 2003
796.72'092—dc22
[B] 2003045149

First Atria Books hardcover edition October 2003

1   3   5   7   9   10   8   6   4   2

ATRIA BOOKS is a trademark of Simon & Schuster, Inc.

For information regarding special discounts for bulk purchases,
please contact Simon & Schuster Special Sales at
1-800-456-6798 or business@simonandschuster.com

Contents

Introduction

A man and his family are standing on top of a twenty-year-old yellow school bus that has been modified with curtains, a rooftop-viewing platform, and a television aerial. According to a friend of mine in the infield who saw it all, the man is at least sixty with a long gray beard and wisps of white hair blowing in the breeze beneath his cap. The cap is black with a white number three on the front, an Earnhardt cap. He wears a black Earnhardt shirt as well, untucked and hanging over his jeans. As I pass through turn three, he stands and applauds. I'm waving, and the man does something completely unexpected. He takes off his cap and bows as I pass: a salute, or at least a show of respect for what we've accomplished.

It's the perfect ending to a perfect day, a day that started like every other Sunday in the NASCAR Winston Cup racing season.

Three nights a week, for thirty-six weeks a year, I sleep in the rear bedroom of a forty-five-foot Marathon motor coach, a custom-designed bus with all the comforts of home. I have a queen-size mattress, three plasma televisions, a couch, a recliner, a full-size shower, and enough of a kitchen to cook pizzas and keep the Pepsi cold. Considering how much traveling I do, this rolling house should be my permanent residence. Virtually every week of the NASCAR season I arrive at the track on Thursday night where the coach is waiting in a reserved section of the infield. I don't drive the coach, which normally tows a Hummer to and from the track. That duty falls to a member of my team named Scott Whitmore. I usually fly into the nearest airport and either rent a car or have Scott pick me up.

By the time I arrive on Thursday, the track looks like it's hosting an RV convention. Some of the rolling houses have been parked in fields outside the track for a week or more. The infield campers file in on Thursday night. That's when the party begins. NASCAR fans are the most dedicated and enthusiastic in all of sports. Stereos blare, kegs are tapped, grills are lit, and the smoky aroma of steaks, burgers, and barbecue drifts through the infield. Imagine a college football tailgate party and multiply it by ten; that's what we have every week. By Sunday morning, the day of the race, many of the fans are partied out. Others are catching their second wind. Either way, it's nice to enjoy a bowl of cereal and watch Speed Channel in relative peace and quiet.

It's the last weekend in October 2001, and we're in Atlanta. I'm up early this Sunday. DuPont, my primary racing sponsor since I began in the Winston Cup series, has a hospitality suite—which is usually a large, lavish infield tent—and I'm scheduled to spend fifteen minutes visiting a group of DuPont customers. At smaller tracks like the one in Martinsville, Virginia, the hospitality tents are in a vacant field outside the track, which makes them hard to get to given the size of the crowds flowing in on race day, but Atlanta Motor Speedway is a big place. I can be at the DuPont suite in a couple of minutes. Then I'll spend a few minutes with a group from my other longtime sponsor, Pepsi, in their hospitality suite twenty yards from the DuPont tent. It's not exactly how I like to spend my mornings, but I understand how important sponsors are to the success of our race team.

It shocks a lot of new NASCAR fans when they learn that drivers schedule sponsor appearances on the day of a big race. I heard one say, "Can you imagine Nike asking Michael Jordan to come by and glad-hand a few execs before game seven of the NBA Finals?" That's what makes our sport so great: the drivers have always been accessible. From my first day behind the wheel of a Winston Cup car, I knew how important my sponsors were to the success of our team, and I've done everything in my power to make sure they're happy with their investment.

I walk into the garage area at around ten forty-five, fifteen minutes before the weekly drivers' meeting that precedes every race. This is where we receive our instructions for this particular day and track, such as where the entry and exit are to pit road. *The entrance to pit road is seventy-five feet in front of the first pit box. The exit of pit road is seventy-five feet beyond the last pit box.* Most of the instructions from NASCAR are the same week in and week out, and most drivers and crew chiefs can recite them from memory.

That said, these meetings are mandatory for drivers and crew chiefs. In today's meeting I see my crew chief, Robbie Loomis, for the first time. He's as good-natured as ever, smiling and speaking to everyone. Robbie and I have become close; we've come a long way together in the last couple of years. I just hope we have a good day today, so Robbie, the crew, and I can add a little icing to the good-size cake we've been baking all season.

If we finish thirty-second or better in today's NAPA 500 in Stockbridge, Georgia, our Hendrick Motorsports 24 DuPont Chevrolet team will win its fourth Winston Cup title, joining Dale Earnhardt and the King, Richard Petty, as the only teams to win NASCAR's highest honor more than three times. Stockcar racing doesn't have a play-off system or a Super Bowl. The best drivers compete against each other head-to-head thirty-six weekends a year at racetracks all over the country. Points are awarded for finishing positions. At the end of the year, the driver with the most points earns the Winston Cup trophy. Winning a lot of races usually translates into winning the championship, but not always; the system rewards consistency. You earn points for leading a lap and for leading the most laps. A team with a dozen or more second-place finishes might earn the most points even if they never win a race. And a driver who wins three or four races but wrecks a dozen times probably won't win the title.

We'd won our fair share of races in 2001, but I've been in this position before, and I know it's never a good idea to get too far ahead of myself. A good finish locks it up for us, and simply starting the final two races secures the championship, but I'm not taking anything for granted, especially this year. This season has been different for all of us. If we win this championship, I know it will be the biggest accomplishment of our careers.

I won my first Winston Cup title at age twenty-four, becoming the youngest champion in the modern era of the sport. That was an emotional time for our team, but even though I knew it was a big deal, a twenty-four-year-old man looks at things a lot differently from someone with a few more years behind him. When I won the title again at age twenty-six and a third time at age twenty-seven, people began to question whether I understood and appreciated what our team had done. Some fans and journalists said I hadn't paid my dues. Others said I wasn't old enough to grasp how tough our sport could be. But they were all saying the same thing: they thought I was too young to get it. I don't believe that was the case; I knew what it meant to be champion, and I was certainly aware of the significance of winning at my age. Still, winning a championship at twenty-four was different from winning at thirty-one. Taking the Winston Cup trophy back to our shop in 1995, 1997, 1998, and finishing second in 1996 was thrilling, but I was young. Every race I won was a joyous experience, but not long after the check presentations and press conferences, I turned my attention to the next week, the next race, and the next goal.

Now, a little older and a little wiser, I see things from a different perspective. This championship will be a first for most of the members of my 2001 team. The crew chief, pit crew, and many of the engineers and support staff weren't with me during our previous three championship runs. They haven't felt the pressure of having a title on the line. They've never known the exhilaration of touching that big trophy, and seeing your name, the car number, and the your team owner's logo engraved in that mammoth wooden base on which the Winston Cup is perched.

I've never seen it the way I see it now, either. Unlike our other championships, I'm now an equity partner, a co-owner of this 2001 team. I've had more input in assembling this team than I've had since the days when my stepfather and I traveled the country towing a sprint car. I've also felt the struggles and the pressures of rebuilding a team, hiring new people, motivating them, teaching them, and keeping them focused on the prize. In previous years, I've been the driver, the "quarterback" of the race team, who leads the effort on race day. Now I'm more involved in all the affairs of the team.

The eyes I look through in November of 2001 have seen plenty of mistakes. At times they've burned with frustration. I have stared into the hearts of good men and asked them to dig as deep inside themselves as they ever have.

Today, they are about to deliver.

Robbie and I, along with twenty or so other drivers and crew chiefs, hang around after the drivers' meeting for the Motor Racing Outreach (MRO) chapel service. Since we travel every weekend, this is the only church service many of us are able to attend. It's always a good one. In the years I've been driving on the Winston Cup circuit, I've seen the services grow from a handful of people to a roomful of drivers, crew chiefs, their families, and usually several hundred fans who stand in the back and worship with us.

After the service, I put on my sunglasses and prepare for the trek back to the transporter that hauls both cars—the primary and the backup—as well as all the parts, the pit box, the uniforms, the radios, the diagnostic computers, a television, a desk, a couple of couches and chairs, lunch, dinner, and just about anything else you might need to run a five-hundred-mile race. The transporter is only fifty yards away, but the walk gets a little tricky, especially in Atlanta where several thousand fans have garage and pit passes—credentials that allow them into the garage and transporter area, as well as up-close access to the pits during the race. More than a hundred people stand between the transporter and me. They're carrying posters, programs, photographs, T-shirts, hats, die-cast cars, and (in the case of some uninhibited women) body parts they want me to autograph. I do what I can to accommodate as many fans as possible, but I can't spend all day here. That's where my PR representative, Jon Edwards, comes in. Jon not only handles all my media requests, he keeps me on schedule. Now he's faced with getting us back to the transporter so I can get ready for driver introductions.

"Okay, I need everybody to stand to one side or the other. Give us a lane," Jon shouts to the crowd. He looks like a Secret Service agent decked out in a black leather jacket with matching slacks and sunglasses. The radio earpiece just adds to his air of importance. It's there for a good reason: he needs to be in contact with the team, and radios are the only way we do that.

Jon does a great job of clearing a path without being too abrasive. It's a fine line. We don't want to offend anyone, but we have to be able to move around. I sign as many pictures and souvenirs as I can while I walk, but it's never enough. I know I've missed somebody who has been waiting all morning to get an autograph. In recent years NASCAR has become more popular than Major League Baseball, PGA Tour golf, ATP tennis, and the NBA, and a big part of that popularity stems from the fact that fans have access to drivers, cars, and teams. But you can only see so many people and sign so many autographs. At autograph sessions for my sponsors we've worked out a system limiting the number of people to two hundred an hour. If I'm scheduled to appear for three hours, the maximum number of people is six hundred. Those six hundred people will get more than one item autographed, get a photo with me if they want, and I can spend quality time with them. Hopefully, everyone leaves the room having had a pleasant experience. Today, there are six hundred people between the transporter and pit road, and I've got about ninety seconds to make that walk. I keep my head up and try to make eye contact with as many people as possible, but I'm sure I miss many. I hope they understand.

By now, 150,000 revved-up fans have found their seats. It's fitting that we have the chance to lock up the title in the town where the first stockcar race was held. I've been told that it was sometime in the mid-1930s when a group of moonshiners carved out a quarter-mile track in a cow pasture a mile away from the current Atlanta Motor Speedway to settle an argument over who had the fastest car. Today, AMS takes up fifty acres and has luxury skyboxes and million-dollar condominiums on the front stretch. Our sport has come a long way.

Once in the transporter I close the door to the lounge, a small area in the front of the trailer with a gray leather semicircular couch, a desk, a laptop, a small closet, and a television. This is my quiet time, the time when I get myself ready for the intensity of the next three hours. I change into my race suit, catch a light bite of lunch, stretch, and tune out everything around me.

Driver introductions are thirty minutes before every race. I gather the team together about five minutes before that. With floor-to-ceiling shelves and cabinets on both sides of the trailer, there's not a lot of room, but the crew manages to cram into the small corridor for a team meeting just before the race. This has become a ritual. At Robbie's suggestion, I started holding these gatherings early in our 2000 season when the team was struggling, and many of the newcomers started questioning what was going on in my head. As we won more races and continued to improve throughout the 2000 season, I decided to continue these sessions. The team needs to know I'm with them. At these meetings, I talk briefly about the week, and any last-minute issues with the car, then lead the group in a short prayer and a chant. These aren't cheers we've memorized; the chants are usually one word or one phrase that represents something we've worked on or a goal we're striving to accomplish at a particular track. The chant changes every week, and it's my way of giving our race-day crew one final "we're in this together" pep talk.

This week I have another message. "We have an opportunity to lock things up today," I say. "But we can't get ahead of ourselves. This is another race. We've run well this week. The car is handling great, and you guys have done an outstanding job."

Like all good crew chiefs, Robbie has learned to anticipate my every word. Still, he remains an attentive listener, especially at these meetings where the crew looks to him for leadership. Cool and collected, Robbie leads by example. He's been the man at the center of a two-year storm during which time he's heard it all. Journalists had been saying that Robbie couldn't step up to the job, that he simply wasn't up to the task of assembling a crew and running a team the way his predecessor, Ray Evernham, had, or that the successes we had achieved in earlier years had all been because of Ray. These criticisms were unfair and unfounded. Nobody's worked harder or is more deserving than Robbie Loomis. Now we're on the cusp of winning another championship, and I can't wait to see what the experts write now.

"We have two races left," I continue. "Let's have a good run. If we do our jobs, everything else will take care of itself." This is code for "Don't focus on the Winston Cup trophy, focus on the race," but I don't need to spell it out for these guys. They're professionals.

"Any questions?" I ask. "Does anybody have anything they want to add?" Nobody does. We all touch hands in a huddle, just like you see on the sidelines of the Super Bowl, and chant, "Finish the job," which is exactly what we have to do.

We're ready to go racing.

— — — —

There are no doors on a racecar. Even though the paint scheme and body design give the impression that my Monte Carlo is just like the one you can buy at your local Chevrolet dealer, that's not exactly the case. Every part, including the chassis, has been manufactured at the Hendrick Motorsports complex in Charlotte according to the NASCAR body template. That's why the Fords, Chevys, and Dodges look so similar. The engine package delivers eight hundred horsepower, and the springs and shocks on all Winston Cup cars more closely resemble what you'd find on a freight train than what your dealer would recommend for the family sedan. The transmission, engine, and steering all have radiators to keep temperatures under control, and the oil tank has its own hundred-ten-volt heating blanket. Every brace, bracket, belt, and bolt is custom engineered, and each part is scrutinized and tested hundreds of times under the most grueling conditions. We have a team of engineers at Hendrick Motorsports who do nothing but analyze data, test tolerances, calculate drag, weight, resistance, torque, and temperature in an effort to squeeze out a few more horsepower.

The interior of the car looks like something out of a gritty science fiction film. Most of the protective cage is exposed so the crew can make visual inspections. There's only one seat, custom molded from foam and aluminum to fit my body. (It would be the ultimate easy chair if it weren't so hard.) The cockpit has a number of gauges and switches that look relatively low-tech; there are no digital heads-up displays, no computer GPS systems; no idiot light telling me my air bag needs attention. There isn't even a speedometer. When you've been racing as long as I have, your butt tells you how fast you're going. The last thing you need is another dial to watch. I have a tachometer, an oil-temperature gauge, water-temperature gauge, and a voltage meter.

The temperature in the cockpit can climb to 120 degrees, so there's a small air hose in my helmet, and with the flip of a switch I can blow fresh air into my helmet and suit. This keeps my carbon monoxide intake to a minimum, and it helps cool me down. It isn't air-conditioning, just outside air venting through the helmet, but it helps. I also have a drink hose in my helmet, a plug for the radio, and a small microphone built into the foam padding near my chin. With earplugs to help muffle the engine noise, I can communicate with Robbie and my spotter, Ron Thiel.

Ron lets me know when a car is on my outside or inside, and when I'm "all clear" to make a move. He also lets me know what other cars are doing and gives me any information he thinks might help me drive the car faster. Ron was a driver; he ran his own Busch North race team before coming on board with us, so he instinctively knows what I'm going through in the car.

Robbie is the same; he and I have developed an almost unspoken form of communication. I tell him what I'm feeling in the car and where I'm feeling it, and he knows what adjustments will make the car faster. It makes him the best crew chief in the business for me.

"Track temp is pretty good," Robbie says, as we're standing beside the car waiting for the national anthem and invocation.

Every car has a sweet spot, a perfect setup for the conditions and the track. Atlanta Motor Speedway is one and a half miles long with twenty-four degrees of banking in the turns, and five degrees of banking in the straightaways, which means drivers have plenty of room to push things. We've chosen a pretty stiff setup, which means the shocks and springs are so firm our truck driver wouldn't even want to put them on the transporter. This allows me to feel every crack and bump on the track. If I were to run over a can, it would feel like I had hit a deer. But that's what is fast these days. This is the fastest track we race on, because it's the longest track and has the highest degree of banking of any long track we run without restrictor plates on the carburetors. That's another difference between my racecar and the Monte Carlo at your local dealership: production cars haven't had carburetors since Kiss had a number one hit.

All forty-three cars are lined up along pit road, and all the teams are standing on the track side of the small wall separating the pit boxes from the pit stalls where the carts are positioned and the tires for the race are stacked. This is where we stand during the national anthem and the invocation, another NASCAR tradition that separates it from other professional sporting leagues. This year these moments of prayer and national reflection are more important than ever. NASCAR has done an admirable job dealing with the tragedies of September 11, making sure our sport is appropriately reverent while knowing our place in the scheme of things. Like other professional sports leagues, NASCAR didn't run any races the week of September 11. We returned to the track twelve days later in Dover, Delaware, with every car displaying the American flag. That week, and every week thereafter, we tried to show our support and pay respect through a moment of silence before each race for those who had lost their lives.

This week in Atlanta is no different. After the invocation we have a moment of silence to honor the fallen Americans from September 11. Seconds later, two B-2 bombers from nearby Dobbins Air Force Base streak overhead.

The racing world experienced another tragedy in 2001. In the first race of the season, Dale Earnhardt was killed when his car crashed into the wall at Daytona International Speedway. Contrary to what a lot of fans believe, Dale and I were friends and business partners. We didn't hunt and fish together, but we had a lot of similar business interests and were close. We talked often and worked well together, had some licensing and mer-chandising deals together, and even owned some real estate to-gether near the Lowe's Motor Speedway in Charlotte. Dale liked to project an image as an intimidator, and plenty of times he made aggressive moves against me on the track, and even more times he jokingly needled me during interviews. But he was also someone I could go to for advice about how things worked, on and off the track, at the top levels of our sport. I never felt any animosity or ill will from him or any member of his team. He raced hard and loved to win. In that respect we were kindred spirits. His death is a terrible blow and a painful reminder of one of the basic truths of our profession: take nothing for granted when you make your living in a racecar.

After the flyby, I start my ritual, the prerace setup every

driver goes through waiting for the words we all love to hear: "Gentlemen, start your engines." Of course it's not as easy as inserting a key and turning the ignition. I climb through the driver's window, then one of my teammates, Jay Lupo, leans in to make sure I'm comfortable in the car. The steering wheel is off its column. This makes it easier to get in and out of the car and get strapped into the seat. Once in the seat, I lock the steering wheel into place, strap myself in with the five-point seat belt, and begin checking the gauges and switches within my reach.

About fifteen seconds before the public address announcer says, "And now for the greatest words in all of sports . . . ," I hit the battery switch to get the electrical systems up and running. Then I flip the switch that operates the tachometer. Next comes the voltmeter switch. With a few seconds left, I hit the crank switch, which doesn't actually start the car, but gets the engine turning over much the way your car takes a few revolutions to turn over when you start it on a cold morning. Finally, when I hear the words "Gentlemen, start your engines," I hit the start switch. The distributor sends power to the engine, and the rumble of a finely tuned racing engine reverberates through my ears. It's become a cliché with all the movies and promotions that play on the theme, but it's true: when forty-three drivers start their engines at the same time, it sounds like thunder. I think it's the sweetest sound in the world.

Jay closes the mesh window net that covers the driver's window and keeps debris from flying into the car, and I rev the engine a couple of times in preparation of exiting pit road and falling in behind the pace car. We start this race in twenty-fourth position, a poor showing by the standards we are accustomed to, but not somewhere I hope to stay for very long.

We started twenty-fourth back in February at the UAW-DaimlerChrysler 400 in Las Vegas and came back to win our first race of the season. If we can't sit on the pole this week, I don't mind a spot that brings back some winning memories.

Dale Earnhardt Jr. is on the pole, having qualified with the fastest time. That means he leads the way behind the pace car and gets his pick of the pits. A lot of times a team's spot on pit road is more important than their starting position. If you have a good car, you can work your way up through the pack during the race. But in the critical seconds of a pit stop when every second counts, having a prime spot can make all the difference.

Our pit isn't bad, but it's not great. We've had worse, and our crew is the best trained, best prepared in the business, so our location doesn't bother me much. We'll work with it.

We run two abreast in the warm-up laps based on how we qualified. The pole sitter is on the inside of the front row, right behind the pace car, and the car that qualified second is to his outside. The third-fastest-qualifying car is on the inside of the second row, and so on. For the fan watching in the stands or on television, it looks as though we're creeping around the track; actually we're going about seventy-five miles an hour. During caution laps, later in the race, we will drive single-file behind the pace car in the order we were in when the caution flag came out. During those laps, drivers weave from side to side (called scrubbing) to keep old rubber from sticking to the tires and to keep them evenly heated. This isn't an issue at the start of the race, so I hold my position and get ready for the green flag. It's impossible to anticipate what I'll do at the start of the race since I have no idea what will happen with the other cars. I use these laps to ramp up my focus.

And then, the pace car exits onto pit road, and we're under way. "Greengreengreengreengreen!" I hear over the headset. The pack of cars speeds up and the jockeying begins. "Outside . . . outside," I hear Ron say over my headset. "All clear."

Starts and restarts are critical. The cars are bunched together, and it's a perfect time to move up a spot or two if you're willing to make a move. I rarely take any big risks early. Track position is always important, but I don't believe in being overly aggressive in the opening lap of the race. Some guys take a different approach and try to move up quickly. I just know from experience that we're out here together for five hundred miles, and there's plenty of time to race.

The crew's done a great job with the car. I jump up three spots on the opening lap, move into nineteenth place by the third lap, and into fourteenth place by the time we run our sixth lap of the day. Now we have a little room. The pack of cars has spread out a little and we have some open air in which to run. From here I can get a feel for how the car is handling when I push it into the turns and which line on the track is the quickest. I can feel the g-forces pulling me to the right, a feeling I've grown used to over the years and one I love. It usually means we're running fast. When we get a few more laps behind us, I'll work on building momentum to push the car closer to the front. Right now, I want to get a feel for how the car is handling. The wind is rushing past, and the cockpit has already heated up to over a hundred degrees. Sweat is pooling in the small of my back as it does anytime I'm in the car for anything longer than a four-lap test run. But I don't really feel it. I'm tuned in to the throaty roar of the engine, and the marks I've picked on the track.

Every track has an optimum line where the car runs at its fastest. That line shifts throughout the race. The car will run one way with a full tank of fuel and another way with less than a full tank because of the difference in weight. It will also run better or worse depending on how fresh the tires are. Then there are the track changes. As the sun shifts and the air and ground temperatures change, the track heats and cools, which will cause the optimum line to shift. Asphalt on a track might start out at eighty degrees Fahrenheit before the first lap of a race, but after twenty or thirty laps, the track temp might be ninety degrees. All those variables, plus the heating up of the tires, cause the feel of the car to change. My job as the driver is to communicate that feeling to the crew chief.

"Little tight on entry, but drive-off's great," I say over the radio. A racecar is tight when it wants to continue going straight after I've turned the wheel. A loose car is exactly the opposite: the rear end of the car wants to turn too much, causing you to spin out. My car is a little tight as I enter the turns, but it's fine through the middle and end of the turn, which I call drive-off. As the track and the tires heat up, the car will loosen up, but as the fuel levels go down and the car gets lighter, it will tighten up even more.

"Okay, Bud," I hear Robbie say. "Your lap times are pretty good." Robbie is sitting on top of our pit cart with a computer in front of him that monitors all my lap times. The transponder tells him how I'm doing compared to the rest of the field.

Carl Long is running twenty-ninth when he spins out and hits the wall in turn two. I'm ahead of the crash, so I'm able to pit as soon the track goes yellow.

"Four tires," I hear Robbie say. "Come right on down, Bud.

Watch Rusty [Wallace] as you turn in." Rusty is in the pit box immediately behind ours.

I turn the car into my pit box, making sure all four tires are inside the yellow paint. NASCAR will penalize a driver who isn't fully in the pit box.

Out of the corner of my left eye I see our jackman, Chris Anderson, come around me like a blur. The right side of the car goes up in one swift, smooth motion, and I see Todd Gantt slide to the ground beneath the fenders of the car. In seven seconds, the right side of the car is down and left side is up. Craig Curione rolls the front tires off pit road while my tire changers work their magic on the left side of the car. Jeff Craven, our gasman, whose other job is to drive the transporter from the shop to the track and back each week, fills the tank with two eleven-gallon cans of fuel. When the jack releases and the car hits the ground, that's my signal. When I hear a "Clear!" that's my signal that no car is right beside me, and I let out the clutch and press the throttle.

"Great job, guys," I say.

I've read that in 1950 the average pit stop took four minutes. By 1980 crews had trimmed that time down to under a minute. During this stop, I'm in the pit box exactly 17.1 seconds. By 2003, we have it down to less than fourteen seconds.

This time in the pits allows me to jump into eleventh place. Once we go back under green, I pass Sterling Marlin to move into the top ten. Tony Stewart and Earnhardt Jr. keep swapping the lead with Ricky Craven, Dave Blaney, and Bill Elliott close behind. With fresh tires I'm able to maneuver through traffic and pass Blaney, Elliott, and Craven. Then on lap thirty-five I take a high line through turn two and pass Stewart to fall into second behind Earnhardt Jr.

"Junior," as he's called in the garage, has had a good year on the track and a devastating year off it. Losing your father is tough under any circumstances (thankfully, I don't know the feeling, yet), but to have your father killed in a race where you are a few feet away from him battling for the win is almost unimaginable. Junior has done a great job of rebounding from that tragedy, and he's become a great competitor. I remember when I first met Junior, he was racing in a late-model series in North Wilkesboro, North Carolina, in a battered old piece of junk I couldn't believe they allowed on the track. I was sitting on the pit wall after practice talking to Dale Sr. when Junior strolled over and Dale introduced us. I remember thinking he looked so young. I ribbed Dale a little bit, saying, "Man, I can't believe you'd put your son out here in a piece of junk like that."

"Hey," Dale said, "if he wants the good stuff, he's going to have to work for it. I'm not going to give it to him just because he's my son. If he proves he's serious, there's plenty of good cars he can drive."

A few years later, Junior won the Busch Grand National series championship. Now, he's leading the NAPA 500 and looking for his third win of the Winston Cup season.

Our lap times are the same as Junior's but he's chosen a low line. My car is a little tighter, and with the track heating up I find the high line working a little better. On lap forty-one, traveling 178 miles per hour with no more than six inches separating our fenders, I'm able to slide by Junior and take the lead.

"Good job, Bud," I hear Robbie say. "That thing looks good out front."

Through sixty laps I've increased my lead to three seconds over a crop of drivers who keep swapping the second and third spots. But the car is tightening up as the fuel load decreases. I hold the lead through seventy-one laps, but I know Junior and Craven have faster cars. In a situation like this, you can play defense, but if you block a guy from passing you for long, he's likely to become impatient and try to move you out of the way. The last thing I need to do this week is crash the car trying to protect a lead I know I can't keep. Craven passes me on lap seventy-two and Junior slips by one lap later.

We pit on lap seventy-six and the crew comes through again, changing all four tires and getting me in and out in great time. That puts me back in second place, six seconds behind the new leader, Tony Stewart, who stayed out while the leaders came into the pits.

Craven and Junior are close behind, and when we hit lap traffic, I'm forced below my high line. "Outside . . . outside," I hear Ron saying. Both those guys pass me again.

Now I have a decision to make. The car is running reasonably well, and I can push my way back into the fray. But we are less than a third of the way into the race. A lot of things can happen in the next two hundred laps. There is no reason to mix it up with Junior and Tony Stewart when the only lap I need to lead is the last one.

I fall back a couple of spots through the next hundred laps, but stay in the top ten, which is good enough to capture the championship. As the fuel levels decrease and the track heats up, the car keeps getting tighter (it doesn't want to turn, and the nose skids up the track a little in the corners), which makes it tough to mount any sort of charge. Plus I'm having trouble seeing. Whatever we've used to clean the windshield has streaked the glass. It's all I can do to fight the glare and debris and see what's in front of me.

That's when I decide we have to be smart. I have a top-ten car, maybe even a top-five car, but the later it gets the more I know we don't have a winning car. There have certainly been times in my career when I've pushed an ill-handling car, when I've taken risks and chosen aggressive tactics to make up for lost time. A younger Jeff Gordon might do that same thing today. But as I've matured and built a bond with my new crew chief and the rest of our team, I've learned that there are days and times to push your way to victory, and times to take the points and enjoy the ride.

Dale Earnhardt was a master at making those kinds of decisions. When we were battling it out for the Winston Cup title in 1995, I was constantly in awe of Dale's ability to analyze a situation and make the right call. Everyone knew him as the Intimidator, a guy who would do whatever it took to win, but he was also one of the smartest drivers I'd ever seen. Dale knew when to push his car to the front of the pack and when to take the points and, in his words, "bring it to the house."

I was fortunate to edge Dale out for the championship that year, and I learned a lot then about racing. Now it's time to apply one of those lessons. A top-ten finish wins the Winston Cup championship. Getting tangled up in traffic and risking a crash because of a grimy windshield doesn't make a lot of sense. This is a day to "bring it to the house."

We make it respectable. I pass Tony Stewart on lap 304 to move into ninth place, then get by Dale Jarrett and Earnhardt Jr. in the last two laps of the race to finish sixth.

Bobby Labonte wins the NAPA 500 when Jerry Nadeau runs out of gas on turn four of the final lap. Once again NASCAR has given the fans a great race with a nail-biting, edge-of-your-seat finish. And my team has won its fourth Winston Cup title.

I've always referred to the 24 car as "my team," an all-encompassing catchall that includes everyone from team owner Rick Hendrick to the guys moving tires in and out of the pit stall and the mechanics and engineers back in the shop in Charlotte. But this is more than "my" team. Robbie Loomis, Brian Whitesell—our team manager—and the rest of the crew who made winning possible are as close as any team in our sport, and I respect each and every one of them. We have had some pretty low points together and endured some brutal criticism. We've struggled through our own doubts, and now we're back on top.

There's a sign below a show car in the lobby of the shop in Charlotte that reads: "Teamwork is the fuel that allows common people to produce uncommon results." Above that sign is a glass case that houses three Winston Cup trophies. Because we believe the words on that sign, we now have a fourth trophy to add to that case.

As I drop the window net and make a victory lap, it starts to sink in. We've done it. We've beaten the odds, defied the critics, rebuilt a team, and become champions again. A lot has changed since I won my first title in 1995, a year we were booed every time we crossed the finish line ahead of Dale Earnhardt, and a year where every week I found myself answering questions about my age, experience, the team, and whether I had paid my dues. Now, as I wave to the crowd at Atlanta Motor Speedway, I sense a shift. There are still a few holdouts, a few diehards holding placards that say things like "Anybody But Jeff" and "Gordon Sucks." A couple of guys give me the one-finger salute as I pass, but those are few and far between. The majority of the crowd stands and cheers.

Among them is the Earnhardt fan standing on the school bus. According to my friend in the infield, he took off his hat and gave a pronounced, ceremonial bow as I passed. It's been a long, hard struggle, a journey that has taken me to the edge of doubt before bringing me back. But earning that fan's respect and the respect of the millions just like him make it all worth it. When I get back to pit road, Robbie is waiting, grinning from ear to ear.

"You did it, Bud. You did it," he says as he helps me out of the car.

"No, you did it," I say. "This one's yours."

"Don't kid yourself. There are more guys like me around to help guys like you, than there are guys like you to help guys like me."

I smile. Typical Robbie. The biggest moment of his career and all he can do is deflect the credit. I don't argue. Deep down I know we're both right.

One

Travel and Leisure

For most of us there is no such thing as typical week for a NASCAR team. My calendar is booked as far as nine months out, and there are few weeks where I can find anything resembling a pattern. I might be testing a car in Rockingham, North Carolina, on a Tuesday and shooting a promotional commercial for Pepsi the Tuesday after that. I could be in the shop meeting with Robbie and the crew this Wednesday, and the following Wednesday I might be in Wilmington, Delaware, for a DuPont appearance. I try to keep my calendar as organized as possible, but the only thing that's certain about my schedule is that there's rarely any downtime.

I try to segment my days into one-hour increments, and as I look at my calendar for the next month, almost every hour is blocked. That's why it's so hard for me to commit to anything at the last minute. The producers of *Live with Regis and Kelly* have asked me several times to fill in for Regis on his show, and while I've been able to do it a couple of times, there have been more times when I've had to turn them down. I use that as an example, because I love doing that show. I have a great time, I always meet interesting people, and it's good exposure for our sport and our sponsors. If I could say yes every time they call, I certainly would. But my commitments are such that I can't.

The only day I block out for myself is Monday. After the conclusion of a race I change out of my race suit, say good-bye to the team, and head to the airport, where I either fly home or scoot off to meet some friends. For the next twenty-four hours I try to do nothing but take care of myself. I might spend the day doing laundry or paying bills. I might go to Lake Norman outside Charlotte, go out on my boat. Sometimes I go to New York. I love the city because my friends and I can walk around, shop, eat, and for the most part be completely anonymous. I also love to dive, so I might go somewhere that I can spend a little time underwater. I bought a new car on a Monday; I do most of my banking on Mondays. Most of the things people do on their weekends or during vacations, I try to squeeze into Mondays.

I try to keep Tuesdays open so I can devote my full attention to those sponsors and media to whom I've committed, whether it's an appearance at a DuPont customer conference or a series of magazine interviews and photo shoots. Unfortunately, I can't say yes to every request. Jon Edwards, who fields most of my media contacts, estimates that I get a hundred requests a week, and he has to turn most of those down because of time. I don't like saying no, but I don't have any choice.

If we've scheduled a test for Tuesday, that's what I do; the car and the team come first no matter what. I'm fortunate to have sponsors who understand that, and they don't mind if I turn down an appearance request because of a test. Getting to Victory Lane is the most important thing for them as well as for us. We try to schedule appearances far enough in advance to avoid any conflicts, but on the few occasions when I'm being pulled in two different directions, our sponsors understand that I'm always going to err on the side of the car and the team.

When I first got in a Winston Cup car in late 1992, I tried to do everything for everybody. If a local reporter wanted an interview, I would call him back immediately and give him as much time as he needed. If a local auto parts store wanted me to do a one-hour appearance, I'd show up and give them as much time as they needed, even if the company didn't sponsor our car. At the time, that wasn't unusual. Most drivers worked out their own one-day or one-hour appearances. We were all trying to grow the sport, and I was trying to get my name out, so we did whatever we could to promote ourselves. A couple of years and a few hundred mistakes later, I realized I was spreading myself way too thin, and doing a disservice to the companies footing the bill for me to go racing. Some of my sponsors saw me doing these one-day autograph signings and wondered why they were writing such big checks when, for a daily rate, I would go anywhere for anybody. Now, I've chosen a few select sponsor/ partners and work with them exclusively. I'm able to give them more time, attention, and exposure, and they don't have to worry about me being overextended and distracted. They're happy, and I'm happy.

That doesn't mean I don't have conflicts. I remember one Monday after a race in Kansas (a race I won), I scheduled a quick trip to Las Vegas for a Warner Brothers movie shoot. I was tired after racing five hundred miles, but the shoot was scheduled for 10 P.M. I figured I'd be on the plane heading home by midnight. What I didn't count on was all of the retakes pushing the shoot back five hours. By the time we started shooting my segment, it was 3 A.M. We finished a little after five, and I got back to Charlotte at 1 P.M. on Tuesday. So much for that day off.

Barring any other conflicts, Wednesday is my day to be in the Charlotte office and race shop. That might mean I spend the entire day meeting with Robbie and our team manager, Brian Whitesell, or I might spend the day with my business manager, Bob Brannan. Fortunately, my business offices are on the second floor of the building that houses the shop for the 24 car and the 48 car (driven by Jimmie Johnson, of which I'm also a co-owner). That puts my licensing operations, my fan club, the merchandizing division, and my foundations offices under the same roof as our mechanics, engineers, fabricators, and pit crew personnel, which works out great for me. I can spend the morning autographing die-cast cars for my foundation, have a quick in-house lunch with my business manager, and spend the afternoon going over next week's race with Robbie and Brian.

While in the Charlotte office, I make it a point to wander around the shop and speak to the guys. I don't intrude, and I certainly don't step on Robbie and Brian's managerial authority, but it's important that everyone in the shop see me and know that I don't just show up at the track on the weekends. I'm still learning a lot about the details of our sport, so it's good that I spend time with the guys who are putting the cars underneath me. I know a lot about the cars (I've been driving and working on cars since I was a kid), but I also know that the technology has advanced beyond my expertise. I rely on our mechanics and engineers to put the best and safest car on the track every week. But it's good for them to know that I'm there for them if they have any questions, or if they need to talk to me about anything.

Late in our 2002 season, for example, one of the guys in our fabrication shop, who also serves on the over-the-wall crew on race day, got an offer to go to another team. Robbie told me about the offer when I was in the shop, and I was able to get with Rick Hendrick and work out a counteroffer that allowed our guy to stay with us. That's part of what I do, now.

That hasn't always been the case. In my early days in Winston Cup, I was the driver and nothing more. The team was employed by Rick and answered to my first crew chief, Ray Evernham. I focused on what I knew, which wasn't running a race team. Now, Robbie and Brian are the bosses who make the day-to-day operational decisions. Rick and I are the co-owners. Someday, when I'm no longer driving, I'll become more involved in the operational side of things. Right now, I'm content to listen, learn, be around when I'm needed, and drive the car.

If a sponsor commitment forces me to miss my Wednesday shop appearance, I'll shuffle things around to be in the office on Tuesday, or Thursday before leaving for the track. I won't schedule a sponsor appearance for a Thursday unless it's on the way to a track. If we're scheduled to race in Talladega, Alabama, for example, and one of my sponsors wants me to appear in Birmingham, I look at that as a great opportunity. But if I'm racing in New Hampshire and the sponsor wants me to travel to Dallas on Thursday, I have to say, "I'm sorry. Hopefully we can do it some other time."

Having my own plane (or, rather, making finance payments on my own plane) helps. I don't have to go through the lines at commercial airports or work my travel around airline schedules. Currently I write checks to the bank for a Falcon 200, a midsize private jet. It's expensive, but when I look at the time I save, and the number of things I'm able to do for our team and for my sponsors because of the jet, I know it's worth every cent.

Usually the plane touches down somewhere near the racetrack on Thursday night, and the rest of my week is spent either driving the car or thinking about the race on Sunday.

— — — — —

The team's schedule is little more predictable, but no less strenuous. The team members who were not at the race the previous weekend (which is about seventy people, far and away the majority of the staff) get to work about six-thirty on Monday morning. At seven, they have a managers' meeting that includes Robbie; Brian; Joe Berardi, our head engineer; Ron Thiel, who, as I've mentioned, is also my spotter; Mark Thoreson, the shop foreman; Pete Haferman, our chief engineer; Wes Ayers, the fabrication shop manager; and Ken Howes, whom we fondly refer to as the "sage from South Africa." Ken, a native of Cape Town, is the competition manager for all Hendrick Motorsports teams, and a guy who knows more about racing than anyone else in the business. Nothing slips by him. Sometimes, especially if there are any big-picture issues to discuss, Rick Hendrick will sit in on these meetings.

At 7:25, the meeting breaks up, and the individual managers have meetings with the men and women in their departments. This is where the managers set the agenda for the day and give the team an overview of what to expect the rest of the week.

The race-day personnel, the guys who go over the wall, and who most novice fans assume compose our entire race team, take Monday off. They usually fly back to Charlotte on Sunday night, or, if the race was close by, they carpool home. Like me, they are usually spent when they hit their pillows on Sunday night. A day of rest and recovery is crucial to keep them fresh and motivated.

As for the bulk of the team—the guys the public never sees, and the ones the novice NASCAR viewer never knew existed, but who are just as important—their hands are full on Monday morning. By eight o'clock, the transporter has pulled into the shop and both cars (the primary car and the backup car from the previous race) have been unloaded. Four men, known as the postrace crew, spend Monday morning stripping the cars, taking out the suspension, removing the engine, washing the chassis, and bringing all the parts into a twelve-by-twenty-five-foot room known as the parts room. All the parts are inspected, cleaned, and serviced. Any unusual damage or wear is logged and reported to the crew chief, and the parts are all tagged for future reference. The suspension goes to another similarly sized room where it's also checked and cleaned.

At the same time, the car body is being washed in the back. After a thorough scrubbing by the crew, the body-shop manager comes out to inspect any damage. Even if I didn't crash the car, there are always dents and dings. A good clean race means we've had lots of fender rubbing and not-so-gentle nudges, all of which leave scars on the car. The body manager notes all of those blemishes and determines which parts must be repaired or replaced.

After a car goes through postrace, it's brought onto the main floor of the shop, where the mechanics put in a new engine and suspension and get it ready for its next outing. A five-hundred-mile race, plus practice and qualifying laps, at 180 miles an hour is all an engine and suspension can take. As for the chassis, the next outing might be in a couple of weeks or in a few months. Most fans know that teams have more than two cars, but I don't think many realize how many cars we have. Before the start of the 2003 season, we had as many as thirty cars (for both the 24 and 48 teams) on our shop floor at once. We have cars for superspeedways, cars for short tracks, cars for intermediate tracks, and cars for road courses. We have six cars specifically for the Daytona and Talladega, even though we only run four races a year at those two tracks. I used to give names to the cars, most starting with the letter *B—Boomer, Backdraft, Beavis, Butthead,* and so on—as a way of personalizing my relationship with the machines. If *Boo* has a good run in Rockingham, it will go through postrace and be set up for its next start, even though that might not be until we go back to Rockingham in three months' time.

On Tuesday morning the over-the-wall crew comes in, and the entire road crew, including the mechanics and the engineers who are at the track Thursday through Saturday, but who aren't a part of the over-the-wall crew on Sunday, meet with the crew chief to go over track notes from the previous race. Tire specialists, engineers, the gasman, the jackman, and all the mechanics go through every detail of the race. Did the tires wear the way we expected? Did the temperatures in the car stay where we thought they would? How did our lap times improve or get worse as we made various adjustments? What were the tire pressures and track conditions when we were running our fastest laps? How fast did we get in and out of the pits, and what can we do in the future to shorten those times by a fraction of a second? All these questions and dozens more are asked and answered during this Tuesday-morning session. Robbie and Brian have televisions and VCRs in their offices so they can view tapes of the race. If there was a screwup, everybody sees it over and over. If we had a particularly good run, it's analyzed and everybody gives input. It's an open and honest meeting, never hostile, with the main objective being to isolate and eliminate mistakes, and to enhance those things we did well.

After the meeting, the pit carts (those large boxes in the pits where the tools and parts are stored and on which the crew chief and the engineer sit during the race) are brought into the gear and suspension rooms. All the parts are removed and replaced with parts needed for the upcoming race. Just as we have different cars for different tracks, we have different parts and tools for different cars. Every drawer and cabinet in the transporter has to be emptied and restocked with the right parts for the week ahead, and the same is true for every square inch on the pit cart.

While part of the crew is setting up the pit carts, the mechanics and the engineers are preparing the primary car. Even though this car was cleaned and reassembled during postrace, the crew chief and engineers work on the skirts, the nose, and the shocks package, all the things we need to set the car up for the conditions we expect at the next race. In addition to being a mechanical genius, Robbie has to be a meteorologist, not to mention a fortune-teller, when he's putting these setups on the cars. If we're racing in Michigan in June, the weather might be sunny and eighty degrees, or it might be forty, cloudy, and miserable. He has to be ready for both, but he also has to set the car up for the conditions he expects when we arrive. Warm temperatures and low humidity might mean a stiffer shock and spring combination and little less air pressure in the tires; a hot, humid day might call for even softer tires, while a cold day might mean softer springs and more air in the tires. Sometimes we get it wrong, but more often than not, the team does a great job getting the car set up pretty close to perfect before it leaves the shop. That comes from years of experience at familiar tracks, and the most detailed notes you could imagine.

Wednesday and early Thursday morning, the crew sets up the backup car. By no later than midday on Thursday, the transporter is loaded and on the road. The early road crew, the mechanics and the engineers who are at the race for qualifying and practice, but are not part of the Sunday over-the-wall crew, fly out on one of the team planes. If they arrive early on Thursday, they check into their hotels and get a bite to eat. I'm usually not far behind. I get to the track around sundown and try to be settled into the motor coach by nine o'clock.

Friday, qualifying day, the over-the-wall guys and the Monday-through-Friday mechanics, fabricators, and engineers stay in the Charlotte shop. The over-the-wall guys might get in a few more practice sessions. We have a mock pit and a car behind the shop with cameras set up to capture every movement from every angle during a pit stop. The over-the-wall crew practices two—and four-tire stops at least twice, and more often three, times a week. The tapes are reviewed, analyzed, and scrutinized just like NFL teams look at game films. When the over-the-wall crew goes home on Friday night, they're ready for the race.

Saturday is practice day at the track, our last chance to fine-tune the car and get it right before the green flag falls on Sunday. It is also the second day off for the over-the-wall crew, although most of them only take a half day off and travel to the track on Saturday night. The Charlotte staff takes both Saturday and Sunday off, which gives everyone at least two days off a week, something I think is important to building a long-term, successful race team. Sure, you can work people twelve hours a day, seven days a week, but not for three or four years. Race mechanics have families, and lives, bills to play, laundry to wash, dogs to walk, and other interests outside of racing. To attract and keep the best people, we've got to be conscious of those personal needs and go out of our way to be accommodating when we can. I think we do a good job at this.

There are exceptions, those weeks when everyone knows they have to pull double duty to get the job done. If we have back-to-back races in Rockingham and Las Vegas, for example, we don't have time to postrace the Rockingham cars and set up the Vegas cars in our standard schedule. It takes two days for the transporter to drive across the country, so the crew has to compress their schedule and set up both Rockingham and Vegas cars the same week. That way when the transporter rolls in on Sunday night, the team can unload and postrace the Rockingham cars and immediately load the Vegas cars while the truck driver gets a few hours' sleep. By late Monday night, the truck is ready to roll west.

No one complains when we work long, hard hours, although I've heard guys from other teams say that NASCAR should rearrange the schedule so we have a break after our West Coat stops. Our team has always adjusted to the schedule. Travel is a small price that we pay for expanding our sport into new markets. There isn't a person in our shop who wouldn't work a hundred hours a week if that was what it took to win. Knowing that fact inspires and pushes me to deliver every week when I get into the car. Everyone involved in the 24 car's crossing the finish line thirty-six Sundays a year—those the public sees, and those who work out of the spotlight in our eighty-thousand-square-foot shop in Charlotte—is critical to our team's success. It's a common saying because it's true: a chain is only as strong as its weakest link.

We travel together, work together, struggle together, lose together, and win together. Sure, I'm the guy the reporters want to talk to on Sunday, and I'm the guy who holds up the giant cardboard checks when we win, but I'm not naive or vain enough to think that I'm the sole reason we're successful. Racing is a team effort—always has been, always will be.

Two

Wonderboy

7 always hated that name. Dale Earnhardt tagged me with it after my first championship in 1995 when I was twenty-four years old, and I still don't know if he meant it as a compliment or a dig. Dale always had a biting sense of humor. He could walk by and cut you with a one-liner without breaking stride while everybody around you was holding his sides and hooting. I've been told that one weekend Kix Brooks (one-half of the country-music duo Brooks and Dunn) was standing in the garage area when Dale walked up behind him and put him in a headlock. Now, here's a guy who makes his living singing; grabbing him anywhere near the vocal chords could be hazardous. But that was just Dale's way of greeting a friend. Another weekend, I heard that Sterling Marlin and his son, Steadman, were eating dinner outside their motor coach when Dale walked by. Without a word, Dale snatched a piece of chicken off of Steadman's plate and kept walking. Dale had never said two sentences to Steadman before that night. The chicken snatch was his way of accepting the younger Marlin into the fold.

With me, Dale was always up-front; he didn't say a lot, but when he spoke, each word had a lot of value. In my first years of Cup racing we talked about business, licensing, appearances, and a lot of the off-track demands of our sport. I also worked on drafting off of Dale during my early practice sessions at Daytona and Talladega. A few years later we worked together to sell our respective merchandising companies to Action Performance, the leading maker of NASCAR merchandise, and we were partners in a real estate deal in Charlotte. Dale was always great to me. But for some reason in those early years, he called me Wonderboy. It was a nickname I would carry for the better part of a decade.

I was used to the names—*kid, boy, squirt,* even a few *punks*—but I always laughed them off. In every car and every league I'd ever raced in, I was always the youngest and the smallest. For a while there it seemed like every race I won I was the youngest winner in the history of the event. I was always the "kid" at every track. When we won our first Winston Cup championship, I was the youngest driver of a championship car since Bill Rexford in 1950.

A lot of people didn't like being beaten by a "wonderboy," and I experienced a lot of jealousy and resentment at every level. The drivers never gave me much grief, but others in and out of the sport weren't as understanding. Whether it was a parent in quarter-midget races (races for kids ages five to fifteen where the cars are a fourth the size of midget racecars) accusing me of lying about my age, a track owner worrying about potential lawsuits and negative publicity if a young kid crashed at his track, or someone accusing my dad and me of cheating, I had to put up with accusations and name-calling from the first day I set foot on a racetrack. After a while I became immune to it. I knew I hadn't done anything wrong, so I tried to laugh it off and go about my business. I figured my fans were going to support me, and those who were fans of other drivers were going to pull against me. That's the nature of racing. The fact that (until recently) I was always the youngest driver in the field just gave those who wanted to pull against me something to base their boos on.

I remember one Sunday in my early Winston Cup days my

mom heard me being booed during driver introductions. Later she asked me, "Why were they booing?" She'll never admit it, but I know it bothered my mom when I was heckled.

"Don't worry about it," I said to her. "As long as they're making noise, I'm happy."

That wasn't an original line. During my rookie year, I watched Dale Earnhardt get booed during driver introductions. I said, "Whoa, what's that all about?" When I asked Dale about it later, he just gave me one of those sly grins of his and said, "As long as they're making noise, I'm happy." That was a great lesson for me, and one I always remember when I hear my name being booed. I know I haven't done anything wrong. The people booing me don't know me personally, so I don't take it personally. They're pulling for their favorite driver. If I'm not him, they're pulling against me. As long as they're making noise and enjoying the race, that's all the matters.

My stepdad, John Bickford, loves to tell a story about when I was growing up and saw Steve Kinser, the best sprint car driver in the world, getting booed. "Why are they booing him?" I asked John.

"They're booing because he wins," my dad said.

According to John, I said, "Well, I hope they boo me someday."

I got my wish, and I haven't minded at all. Winning is a great feeling, even if you are getting heckled.

– – – – –

I learned to love winning early in life. In fact, I can't remember a time when I wasn't competing in something and trying to beat the guys next to me. When I was four, it was BMX racing at a track near our home in Vallejo, California. Like most kids, I got a bike when I was young, but unlike the other four-year-olds in the neighborhood, I wasn't into training wheels and casually cruising the cul-de-sac. I figured if you could ride something, you could race it, which is exactly what I did. I also picked up on things pretty quickly—and still do to this day. If I'm given a little time with something, whether it's a video game or a new sport I'm learning, I can usually pick up on it relatively quickly.

When I was five, John took me to the local BMX track in the afternoons, where I lined up and ran with kids who were much bigger than me. Mom said I looked like a baby out there, which wasn't far from the literal truth. I was always a small kid (at five feet eight inches I'm not exactly a giant now), so when I was four, I looked like a two-year-old. I didn't care. The speed didn't bother me, and when I realized I was just as good as the older kids, I wanted to spend every spare minute racing. Winning was fun, even for a kid who could barely read the words on the trophies he was getting.

My mom wasn't thrilled. "John, we can't let Jeff race with those kids," she said.

"Why not?" John said. My dad loved racing of any kind, and he saw nothing wrong with a boy exercising his competitive skills on a track.

"Because it's dangerous!" Mom said. A couple of days before this conversation, one of the older kids I had raced against broke his arm in a bike crash, and several of the kids were already wearing knee braces from previous accidents. Mom was all for letting me have some competitive fun, but the thought of rushing her baby to the emergency room with a broken bone or worse was frightening. She put her foot down; no more BMX racing.

I don't remember any of those discussions, because my mom and dad were careful to keep adult conversations out of earshot. My sister, Kim, is four years older than me, so I have a feeling she knew more than I about the BMX negotiations, but she never said anything. All I know is, one day John came home from work with a flatbed trailer hooked to the back of his car. On the trailer were two quarter-midget racecars.

This was like Christmas for me. I jumped up and down and couldn't wait to get behind the wheel. Mom's reaction was a little different. "Are you crazy?" she said to John. "I think bicycles are too dangerous, so you put him in a car!"

I was too busy checking out the car to pay attention to the conversation, but Mom and John have recounted it enough times that I know what was said.

"Calm down," John told her. "A bike has two wheels, and this has four; he's strapped into the car; there's a roll cage around him, and he'll have a full-faced helmet. Kids aren't going to run over him in a car, even bigger kids. This is safer."

John had obviously crafted this argument in his mind on the way home. He did a good job. Mom wasn't immediately convinced, but it didn't take long for her to come around, especially when she got behind the wheel of the second quarter midget and ran around a little makeshift track with me.

Years later I heard John explain the situation like this: "I found a guy named Paul Stornetta in Napa, California, who had two cars, a trailer, a spare motor, and some extra tires, most of which were junk. I bought out everything he had for four hundred fifty dollars. One of the cars had originally been red, but it had been sitting in a barn for so long it had faded to pink. It was a little bigger, so everybody assumed I'd bought one car for you and one for Kim. We're a close family, and we share, so that was a reasonable assumption. But I never thought Kim would race. She wasn't that kind of personality. I simply bought everything Paul had and assumed I could rob parts off one of the cars to keep the other one running."

For the record, my car was black. I never even sat in the pink car.

John was a race junkie. He followed the sport the way baseball fanatics read the box scores every morning and know who's got the best minor league prospects. He took my mom to a race for their first date. Kim was five and I was one at the time, and my mom was working at a hospital supply company to support us. John designed motorized vehicles for handicapped folks, so he met Mom through work. They were married when I was very young, so as far as I was concerned, John was my father from the get-go.

I guess if he'd been a horse trainer, I might have grown up to be a jockey, or if he'd been an avid golfer, I might be trying to compete against Tiger Woods (if he'd been John Wooden, I'm afraid the NBA would have been out of the question). But John was none of those things; he was an engineer who built parts that allowed handicapped citizens to drive cars. He also built racing parts on the side. It was no surprise to those who knew him when he came home that day with a couple of racecars.

John and my mom are always asked if I was a child prodigy. I've never been sure how you define that, and since I'm not a parent, I don't feel qualified to answer. The only thing I can say is that Tiger Woods might have shown some talent and aptitude for golf when he was a kid, but if Earl Woods hadn't taken him to the driving range every day, Tiger might be working in the marketing department at Nike rather than being one of the company's star athletes. Dan Marino's father was his football coach; Barry Bonds's dad was a major league player and manager. No matter what you think of him, Richard Williams made Venus and Serena what they are today. In racing, legacies are almost a prerequisite. Earnhardt, Petty, Fittipaldi, Foyt, Mears, Andretti, and Allison: these are all family dynasties in our sport. As I've heard John say a hundred times over the years, "Kids don't come out of the womb with their future occupation stamped on their foreheads. You're a product of your environment."

My environment was racing. From the time I was five years old, every minute I wasn't in school was devoted to either driving a car, working on a car, traveling to and from a track, or thinking about how to make a car go faster. John would come home from work and the two of us would drive fifty miles to a track where I would run dozens of practice laps. John would stand beside the hay bales holding a stopwatch while I drove. "Okay," he'd say. "Was that lap better, worse, or the same as the one before?"

"Better," I'd say.

"No, Jeff, it might have felt better, but you were three-tenths of a second slower."

I caught on pretty quick. We'd work for hours—one lap, two laps, better, worse, same—then John would drive back home while I slept in the backseat.

On Fridays, we would load the trailer and go racing. At first, I had trouble controlling the car. I would get excited when the green flag fell, and before I knew it, I was spinning into the hay bales. "It's okay," Dad would say. "But going fast doesn't mean anything if you don't finish the race. You've got to push it, but you've got to be patient."

I'm proud that I catch on to things as quickly as I do. Once I got my head around what John was telling me, I started winning races, and the feeling was overwhelming. Even for a five-year-old, the adrenaline rush of driving a racecar and taking the checkered flag was about as thrilling as it got. My confidence grew every week, and we got on a roll where I won a lot of races and a local quarter-midgets championship by the time I was six.

I also realized that as much as I loved winning, I had an equally intense hatred of losing. When I was six years old, a kid named Ricky Patrussi lapped me at a Baylands race. As we were driving home that night, I told everyone in the car, "I never, ever, ever want to be lapped again."

In 1979, John moved us to the national quarter-midget circuit, where we raced every week. I set eight track records that year and won fifty-two times on that circuit, which prompted the first accusations of cheating. People accused my dad of rigging a hot car (one that fudged the rules of weight and balance). It was a charge we would hear throughout my career, including in Winston Cup.

"If you believe that," John would say, "I'll sell you this car."

He did just that, taking home a tidy profit in the process.

"But, John, I liked that car," I'd say.

"Don't worry," he'd say. "I'll build you another one just like it." The following week, we'd win again, leaving the buyer of our old car scratching his head.

Looking back on those days, it's hard to fathom the commitment my mom and dad made when I was five, six, seven, and eight years old. We traveled and raced every single weekend for more than two straight years. Every spare penny was poured into parts for the car, entry fees to races, travel, lodging, meals, gasoline, whatever we needed for me to race.

"If you'd have seen how much money we poured into a five-year-old, you'd have said we were crazy," I've heard John say in recent years. "At first Jeff showed no talent at all for racing. But I've always believed that a lot of people wait to see potential in a kid rather than developing that potential. Jeff had good reaction time and coordination, and more than anything else, he had an innate ability to concentrate, more so than you would find in a normal five-, six-, or seven-year-old. Plus, he listened to me, which was something unique. Maybe it was because I was the stepfather, so he paid a little more attention. But there were still times when he wanted to do other things instead of race."

John is very open about his motives in those early years. "I grew up in a family of ten," he says. "We didn't have enough money for me to do what Jeff got to do when I was five years old. So a lot of this is about me living a second childhood."

By the age of twelve I'd won over two hundred races and done just about everything you could do in quarter midgets and go-karts. In speedway karts I won a lot of races. I also continued to run quarter midgets. John moved me to karts so I could learn to race faster cars that required more driving skill. There are no suspensions on karts, the tracks are much bigger, and the speeds are faster than quarter midgets. I continued to race well, and win, but when you're twelve years old, and on the verge of adolescence, you start looking for other things in life. I got bored.

A lot of people thought our racing was more about John reliving a childhood than about me, but I never thought that was the case. When I wanted to do something else, my mom and dad supported me.

"How about waterskiing?" I asked when I was twelve. It looked fun. It was fast, it was in the water, and you got to do cool tricks.

"You sure you want to do that?" John said.

"I'd like to give it a try."

So we tried waterskiing. John went after that sport with the same gusto he'd shown with my racecars. He enrolled me in professional ski schools and got me in front of all the right people, which was something he was a master at doing. I'm sure if I'd been a singer, he would have gotten me in front of the dean of Juilliard before my thirteenth birthday. It didn't matter what the discipline was, Dad worked every angle to make sure I had every opportunity to succeed.

For most of the summer of my twelfth year I worked on waterskiing, learning to slalom and do tricks on the water. But I could never get the hang of jumping. I've never been a big fan of flying through the air. I don't know what it is that makes me uncomfortable, but I just can't let my body relax and let go to make those jumps. I loved slalom, but without jumping I wasn't going to be much of a competitive skier. Plus, I learned pretty quickly that to be competitive in the slalom, you needed to be tall. Long arms and legs are a big advantage, and I knew I was never going to have either.

I could still have fun with it (and I still do), but it wasn't something I could devote a lot of time and energy toward, because I knew I couldn't be competitive.

This was a critical juncture in the early part of my racing. I'd done everything I could do in the two classes of cars where most of the kids my age competed, and at twelve, I was getting into trouble. It was nothing earth-shattering, just the normal things adolescent kids go through. I started hanging around with some guys who were into mischief, and I found that I liked being a little bad with them. If I hadn't progressed in my racing, and if I had continued to fall in with the crowd I was hanging out with at the time, I could have gone down a very bad road.

My mom and dad recognized this. They knew I needed to fill my time with something other than hanging out with future hoodlums. I needed to take the next step in my racing. Unfortunately, it wasn't clear what that next step was. In California, there weren't a lot of cars I could drive at ages twelve and thirteen.

Then I read a story in a racing magazine about a thirteen-year-old kid named Sport Allen who was racing sprint cars.

— — — — —

Going from a go-karts and quarter midgets to seven-hundred-horsepower sprint cars was a huge jump. I'd always been a big fan of the World of Outlaws racing series where guys like Steve Kinser, Brad Doty, and Jack Hewitt burned up tracks around the country and put on a heck of a show. If you were a kid looking to work your way up in open-wheel racing, these were the guys you wanted to copy. They were tough men driving tough machines, raw, straight-line-acceleration vehicles with lots of power and a nagging tendency to get away from the drivers. You can flip a sprint car faster than you can sneeze, and you're usually traveling at a healthy speed when you do it. They are fast, hungry, primal cars, and I couldn't wait to try to drive one.

There were a lot of discussions at home. Was I sure this was what I wanted? Did I realize the leap I was making? Was I sure I didn't want to try full midgets? Did I understand the commitment I had to make? Could I physically do it? And most important, would anybody let another thirteen-year-old kid race such a powerful machine?

I couldn't answer every question, but I told my parents I was ready to go sprint car racing. So John and I paid a visit to Lee Osborne in Jamestown, Indiana. Lee built sprint cars out of a shop near Indianapolis, the mecca of open-wheel racing, and a place I would soon know well. We must have looked like quite a pair walking into Lee's shop. John asked him about buying a used motor and a sprint car chassis. Lee's forehead crinkled, and his eyes narrowed as he cocked his mouth into something between a smirk and a smile. "You're a little old to be getting in a sprinter, aren't you?" Lee said to John.

"It's not for me," John said. "It's for Jeff." He pointed to me, a thirteen-year-old who looked about eleven.

Lee's eyes went from narrow slits to giant ovals. His hands went up and his head shook quickly. "No way, uh-uhhhh. I'm not building a sprinter for a child. That's ridiculous. What, are you crazy?"

I expected John to get a little defensive, but he obviously expected this reaction. He stayed calm and smooth, but firm, just as he did when he spoke to me on the track. "Certainly that's your right," John said, "but let's talk about it first." John filled Lee in on everything I'd done, but Lee wasn't budging. We headed back to California with only a promise that Lee and John would talk again in a few days.

The phone lines were hot in our house for the next forty-eight hours. John wasn't about to take no for an answer, and Lee was hard to convince that building a sprint car for a thirteen-year-old was a good idea. Almost nobody driving sprint cars was under eighteen. John talked Lee through the liability issues. We would bear full responsibility for anything that happened to me in the car. Lee was also worried about his reputation. It was one thing for a father living a second childhood to put his son in a seven-hundred-horsepower rocket, but it was something else for a seasoned professional racecar builder to give them the tools for such madness. Eventually, and I'm not even sure how, John convinced him that when I started winning, Lee's reputation would be safe.

Then there was the issue of money. We didn't have a lot, and at the time sprint car motors ran upward of $40,000. But John was savvy; not only did he convince Lee Osborne to build a chassis for us, he convinced him to do it on trade for racing parts that John manufactured in his shop. He then sold our boat (no more waterskiing trips for a while) and raised enough money to buy a used motor, which he assembled and installed. In one month, we went from having no car and no prospects, to being ready to go racing for under $10,000. The only hiccup was the seat; I wasn't your average-size sprint car driver, so John had to build a special seat so I could reach the pedals and steer.

Our second problem was finding a place for me to drive. I couldn't race or even test sprint cars in California until I was sixteen. John and I immediately broke the law by going out to a narrow gravel road east of Vallejo where I could learn a few things about the car. "We've got to make sure you can start this thing," John said. You have to push-start sprint cars, and there is a fuel switch I needed to hit. When we got out on the road, I hit the fuel switch and the car started, and I thought it was going to jump off the road. Man was it powerful! The quarter midgets I'd been racing had a 2.85-horsepower engine. The go-karts had a ten-horsepower. My sprint car had seven hundred horses and would go from zero to sixty in a shade under three seconds. It topped out at 135 miles per hour, but it would hit a hundred faster than a Porsche. For me it was like going from a single-engine Cessna to an F-16.

Plus, I was going to race this car without ever having tested it. In Vallejo, all I'd learned how to do was start the car. My first experience behind the wheel of a sprint car would be in the practice session of my first race.

John walked me through the process: "When you're driving a faster car, you have to pick your marks farther down the track." This was a concept I'd learned making the jump from quarter midgets to karts. The faster you go, the farther out you have to focus to make those adjustments. Usually you do this without thinking about it. You're driving along at fifty miles an hour looking at certain spots on the road, and when you accelerate to seventy, your field of vision expands a little bit because you're getting to your marks a little faster. For me, that transition was about to become much more dramatic. I'd been sliding around a go-kart track at forty miles an hour; now I was pushing triple digits.

After doing nothing more than starting the car, John and I loaded up in our trusty trailer and headed twenty-five hundred miles east for Jacksonville, Florida. It was February 1985, and I was about to be indoctrinated into the world of big-time racing.

John chose Florida because they had something called Speedweeks, an All-Star sprint car series on two different tracks in Jacksonville and Tampa with no minimum age requirement. It was great opportunity for me to get some good competitive races under my belt at a spot where I could get used to the tracks. If it had only been one race, it wouldn't have made sense to drive across the country, but because we had five races on two tracks, I could get a feel for the tracks and the surroundings while I was racing. John called the organizers and got the go-ahead for me to race. Sport Allen, who was now fifteen, had already driven several races and was being written about in *Open Wheel* magazine, so I felt confident that we would be accepted. It wasn't like I was breaking new ground.

You don't realize how big this country is until you've driven across it. I didn't think we were ever going to get to Florida. Heck, I didn't think we were ever going to get out of Texas! We got to Jax Raceway tired, dirty, hungry, and ready to race.

That's when the trouble started. When we checked into the hotel where all the racers were staying, a few people asked John if he was driving the car. He said, "No, Jeff is," pointing to me. That earned us a lot of stares. By the time we got to the track and began unloading the car, word had already spread that a kid who looked about ten was going to drive. I could sense we were in trouble before we unloaded the trailer. There was a buzz at the track, and we were at the center of it. We hadn't been in Jacksonville an hour when a fellow named Bert Emrick, the head All-Star official, came out and approached John.

"Who's driving this car?" he asked.

"Jeff is," John said, pointing to me.

Bert's mouth contorted into the biggest frown I'd ever seen. "Noooooo way!"

"Hold on a minute," John said. "I spoke to you before we

left California and I told you about Jeff and his age. We had an agreement, and we've driven three thousand miles to race based on your word."

Bert rubbed his chin, kicked the asphalt, walked around, and frowned some more. He'd known I was thirteen, but he hadn't expected me to be so small. I'm sure I could have gotten the ten-and-under discount at the local theater, and the last thing Bert wanted was a child who wasn't capable of driving the car to get hurt in his event.

John later told me that some of the adults actually accused him of child abuse to his face. I didn't hear those comments, but I could sense that they thought my dad had pushed me into this sprint car. In fact, John had gone out of his way to make sure this was what I wanted to do, and that I was as prepared as I could be. If I hadn't been ready, he would been the first to say, "Jeff, I think we need to take a different route." Instead, he had flown to Indiana, negotiated his heart out to get Lee Osborne to build a sprinter for me, put the motor in the car himself, built a seat so I could drive, taken me out on that dirt road and risked getting into serious trouble with the California Highway Patrol so I could at learn how to start the car, and then taken time away from his business to drive from one coast to the other.

All I wanted was a chance to see if I could drive this new type of car in competition, and these folks were acting like I was being abused by the man who had made this dream possible. "Just let your driving do the talking," John said. He was right. Assuming they let me drive the car, the best course of action was to stay quiet and let my performances on the track speak for themselves.

Just as he wore Lee Osborne down, John did a masterful job

of bringing Bert Emrick around. We could race in the All-Star series as long as we signed a liability waiver and started in the back of the pack.

That afternoon I was suited up and in the car, idling around the track waiting for the green light to flash so we could run some hot laps. When the lights went green, I felt like I was trapped in a *Star Wars* video game. Guys were flying by me faster than anything I'd ever seen. My whole body shook as those cars sped by me. It scared me to death; this wasn't go-karts anymore. Guys like Doug Wolfgang and Bobby Davis Jr. were in the field, seasoned pros who were out there to win. If that meant running over a thirteen-year-old, so be it. When I finally did get in the gas a little bit, the car shot forward like I'd just punched the afterburner button. I did my best to hold the line, but the back end got a little loose and my right rear tire scraped the wall.

When I got back to the pits, I shouted at John, "You lied to me! You said they weren't that fast!"

"Calm down," John said. "You got in the throttle a little quick, but other than that you did fine." He had a great knack for calming me down and keeping me on an even keel. Still, I wasn't so sure this sprint car thing was right for me. That first night I was in over my head, and I knew it.

Fortunately, the race got rained out so I had time to relax, regroup, and get myself mentally ready for the next four races at East Bay Raceway in Tampa. I also realized why John had chosen this All-Star Circuit of Champions series. As he would explain later, "I wanted a spot where Jeff could race several nights in a row so he could get used to one track. I wanted him to get better each night racing the same guys on the same surface, and also get used to the peer pressure. By putting him in a familiar setting four nights in a row, I thought I could eliminate some of the distractions and give him a better opportunity to perform."

We didn't win any of those races. We didn't even make it to the Main Race any of the four nights. But by the third night, I was a lot more comfortable in the car. I finished fifteenth and eighteenth in the B Main race the final two nights, and I qualified eighteenth out of fifty-four cars, just four-tenths of a second behind the top qualifier. That was good enough for me to win my first racing purse from a professional series. It was a little more than $300, and it was cool to walk up the pay window, give them my car number, and have them count out our winnings in cash. It was barely enough to cover our hotel bill in Tampa and the gas we'd spent driving there, but as far as I was concerned, it was the most important money in the world. People were actually willing to pay us to race. For a while that was a concept I had a hard time grasping, but it didn't get much better than that.

I also got my first taste of the national media that week. Somebody alerted ESPN that a thirteen-year-old kid was in the field, so they shot some footage. When I finished well the final two nights, I was featured on the network's *Speedweeks* program.

Once school was out, my dad and I hit the road with the sprint car. We were at a different track in a different town throughout the Midwest every week all summer. I raced in twenty-two All-Star events that first season and made the A Main race twelve times, finishing twelfth three times. I also ran a few non-All-Star sprint races where I did quite well. I had two second-place finishes at the KC Raceway in Chillicothe, Ohio (the track where I would win my first sprint car race a year later), and another second at Bloomington Speedway in Bloomington,

Indiana. That race in Bloomington was pretty special to me because when we arrived at the track, Lee Osborne was waiting for us. He offered to help John set my car up for the race, and he offered some insider tips for running the track. Lee's presence was a nice tribute. We hadn't won the world over yet, but we had made a believer out of Lee Osborne. That was a step in the right direction.

— — — — —

Later that same year, 1985, my parents made another decision that astounds me in retrospect. John and I had traveled the country like a couple of nomads for most of the year, and I'd missed more than a few days of eighth grade to the dismay of my teachers and friends. In California, you aspired to be an actor or a football star. When you told your friends you wanted to be a racecar driver, you got a lot of sideways glances. The culture of American racing was still firmly rooted in the Midwest and the Southeast. I loved our town and my friends, but at the time California was no place for a teenage racecar driver; I couldn't even race in my own state. So my mom and dad decided we would move to Indiana, where open-wheel racing is the state sport, and schoolchildren learn the names of past Indy 500 winners before they learn the capital of Montana.

The decision made perfect sense at the time. My sister graduated from high school in the spring of 1985, and she was on her way to San Diego State in the fall. I was transitioning from middle school to high school, so if we were going to make a move, this was the perfect time to do it. Plus, my parents were concerned about the crowd I had begun to hang out with in

California. If we stayed in Vallejo, I might fall in with the wrong kind of people and get in a lot more than just mischievous adolescent trouble.

I don't remember the move as that difficult a decision, which, in hindsight, is astonishing. As an adult I've moved enough times to know what a major pain it is. Now, in my thirties, it's hard to imagine uprooting and leaving a family business in the hands of others so a fourteen-year-old can have more opportunities to race. But it was no big deal for my parents. They always put my sister and me first (Kim might say that my racing always came first and she came second). Moving to Pittsboro, Indiana, just outside of Indianapolis, made sense for my racing, so that's what we did.

The move brought financial hardship. Mom bought the house in Pittsboro, a small farming town about twenty miles west of Speedway Boulevard in Indianapolis, while John and I were off racing. We didn't even see the place until she'd signed a contract. Then, John and I moved while my mom stayed in California, ran the business, and sold our house in Vallejo. By the time John and I hit the road again for my second season of sprint car racing, we were stretching every dollar we could scrounge. John would make deals and trades for parts and tires, and we would put any decal we could on the car if somebody was willing to cut us a deal on fuel or tires or a free lunch or two. We had to be cost conscious, but John never wavered or complained. We were where we were because we wanted to be there.

Fortunately, I started running really well. I won my first race that second year in Chillicothe, but the race that stands out most in my mind was back in Florida at the Tampa Fairgrounds during Florida Speedweeks. This time there were no problems with the All-Star officials. I made the feature event four out of five races that week and finished in the top twenty every race. But in the last race, the one at the fairgrounds, I started up front and was leading well into the latter half of the race. This was significant because the guy right behind me was Steve Kinser, my boyhood idol and the undisputed King of the World of Outlaws. Steve passed me in the final laps, and I finished fourth.

Afterward, Steve marched down the garage area and found me. I thought, "Uh-oh, what have I done?" When he got to me, he shook my hand and said, "Kid, you're going to be a good one." After all the titles I've won and all the things I've accomplished in racing, that compliment from Steve Kinser still ranks as one of the highlights of my racing career.

Sprint car racing was a lot more fun once I started winning. Winning is what has always driven me. If I never won, I would give up racing and move on to something else where I could be competitive. In five years of running sprinters I won a lot of local races, an All-Star race, four races in the USAC Sprint Car series, and I had three top fives in the World of Outlaws. I also got to make a couple of overseas trips when a New Zealand car owner named John Rae flew my family and me down to Australia and New Zealand for a series of races. The first trip to Australia was great, but I didn't run very well. The second trip, where we ran in New Zealand, we were picked up in a limo at the airport and put up in a suite (both things I'd never experienced before) and generally treated like royalty the whole time we were there. What made it even more of a treat was that I won almost every race. We ran fifteen races in New Zealand during that two-week stretch, and I won fourteen of them. It certainly made the trip worthwhile.

Fortunately, I had my friends in Pittsboro to bring me back down to earth. There's nothing like third-period biology on a Monday morning to add a little perspective to a successful race weekend. I was lucky in that regard, too. Most of my teachers at Tri-West High School followed racing and knew what I was doing, so they understood about missed classes and sleepy Mondays. One of my teachers, Steve Williams, was an avid race fan, so he turned my science projects into modified race projects. Combustion in a race engine, propulsion, velocity, mass, resistance, all the stuff that bores kids to tears was turned into race-themed learning experiences. I also had plenty of friends in school to keep me grounded. A good high school friend, Todd Osborne (Lee's son), and I worked on cars, chased girls, played video games, and got into trouble after school, proving I was just as capable of mischief in Indiana as I was in California.

One of the questions I'm asked more than any other is if I somehow feel cheated out of a childhood. Not only is the answer absolutely not, I'm always a little surprised by the question. Before my eighteenth birthday, I won six hundred races, traveled to the other side of the world, drove almost every square mile of this country, met thousands of people, learned about business, economics, marketing, sales, and the value of relationships—all while doing the thing I wanted to do more than eat, drink, or breathe. To somehow think I missed out because I didn't cruise the Dairy Queen or go to the Tri-West High School basketball games on Saturday nights is not to understand me. Sure, I didn't hang out at the mall as much as some of my friends, and I missed the Friday-night dances in the local gym, but if I had missed one race to go to a football game or a dance, I would have been miserable. Did I have a "normal" childhood? It was normal for me. I couldn't imagine it any other way.

Another thing I learned was the value of sponsorships, and the responsibility that comes with driving the car for another owner. As I became more competitive and started winning more races, car owners approached John about having me drive for them. This was great. Sure, we were bringing in some money for our finishes, but John had nothing in the way of sponsorships and we were running every weekend on a shoestring. The first owner I drove for, Marshall Campbell, owned a red number 20 sprint car. (In fact, I'd raced against his car several times.) One week his driver was unavailable, so he went to John and said, "What do you think about Jeff driving the car for me?"

My dad said, "Sure, we'll drive the car for you." John was always part of the deal. He was my mechanic, crew chief, business manager, and coach. Wherever I went, John went, too.

We won the race in Marshall Campbell's car. When his driver came back the following week, I was teased mercilessly for winning a race one week and getting fired the next.

For the next couple of years, we were in hot demand. Gary Stanton had a car that had just won the King's Royal, and he asked if I would sign on with him for three races, which we did. Then we drove for an owner named Terry Winterbothum for a couple of years. Eventually, we settled on an owner named Rollie Helmling, which allowed us to expand into the Midget series as well as the dirt cars. Fortunately we won in all three, which made for a hectic schedule, but it was all worth it.

One of the first races I ran for Rollie was the 500 Mile Race at Indianapolis Raceway Park, the night before the Indy 500. I was anxious to do well to impress my new car owner; plus, the race was televised on ESPN. A lot of racing fans would hopefully be seeing me for the first time. When I won that race, it did a lot for my confidence.

Rollie was a big-time operator in Midget cars, with RC cola and, later, Diet Pepsi as his sponsors. For the first time in my career, I was asked to be part of a promotional photo shoot for a sponsor. This was something different, but I was prepared. My parents had always taught me to be gracious in every situation, but to go out of my way to be available for someone who was helping me. In the early days when my dad was funding everything, Hoosier tires, worked with him on financing and price breaks, and we went out of our way to thank them every week. If a reporter wanted to know the details of a race, I would start by thanking everybody who had made it possible, including Hoosier tires, who had given us a chance to run that week. I'm sure it sounded like shameless promotion, but without those guys we couldn't have competed, so I thanked them every chance I got. And I carried that attitude and sense of graciousness with me to Rollie's team. We won fifteen USAC National and Western States races in Rollie's car, along with a national title, and I went out of my way to thank Rollie and our sponsors after every win.

— — — — —

In 1990, my career took another fateful twist. I had just won the USAC Midget Championship and I was looking to move to the next level. The only question in my mind was, what was the next level? In open-wheel racing (where the cars have no fenders), the ultimate American ride was with an organization called

CART (Championship Auto Racing Teams, sometimes called Champ Cars). These were the cars in the Indy 500 driven by legends like Rick Mears, Parnelli Jones, Johnny Rutherford, Mario Andretti, and A. J. Foyt. The other option was Formula One racing, an international league that is the most watched in the world. Even with the explosive growth of NASCAR in recent years, F-1 is still the most recognized and watched auto racing on the planet. More people watch an F-1 race on any given Sunday than watch NASCAR in an entire season. The problem with moving into F-1 was logistics. I'd have to move to Geneva, London, or Monte Carlo, and I'd probably have to learn to speak French, German, Spanish, and Italian, none of which appealed to me at the time.

The other problem with moving up in any open-wheel series was availability. Starting in the mid-eighties, CART and other open-wheel divisions experienced a priority shift. A lot of drivers (many of them from Europe and South America) bought their way into the driver's seat by bringing sponsors with them. Suddenly, a team owner who was looking to fill a seat had a crop of skilled drivers at his disposal, some of whom came with large six-figure sponsorship checks. I'd met a few midlevel marketing managers at Diet Pepsi, and I knew the guys at Hoosier Tire pretty well, but that was it. I didn't have anybody willing to write a huge check so I could go shop a ride. Sure I had a lot of wins, and a great reputation, but that and a gallon of methanol would get me a smile and a wave on my way out the door. I needed to broaden my options.

I had one good opportunity with an owner named Cal Wells to race a Toyota truck in a Stadium Truck series. Cal flew me to California to test one of the trucks, which I promptly flipped and rolled three times. Ivan Stewart from Toyota tried to sound positive about the situation, but I assumed my career with Cal and Toyota was being dragged off to the scrap yard with the truck I'd just totaled. To my surprise, Cal continued to call, which was flattering, but ultimately we weren't able to work out a deal.

That was when John and a friend named Larry Nuber (who was also providing racing commentary for ESPN) suggested that I try the Buck Baker driving school in Rockingham, North Carolina. At the time the only thing I'd driven with fenders was my Chevy pickup. Racing a stockcar was something new and different. I wasn't sure how I would like it, but I was willing to give it a shot. What I didn't know at the time was that Larry had worked out a deal with Buck. If I attended, ESPN would come down and do a feature on the school and me. So Larry convinced Buck that a spot on ESPN was worth the price of admission. I got the school for free; Buck got a five-minute plug on ESPN. Little could any of us have known what a turning point that week in North Carolina would be.

Buck was a legendary stockcar driver, someone I had read about and looked forward to meeting. My mom traveled with me because I wasn't old enough to rent a car or a hotel room. I was excited in the same nervous way I was before my first sprint car race. I knew this was something big and new.

After my first day at the school I knew where my future was. I loved stockcar racing. It was the first time I'd raced anything that big, heavy, and full-bodied. The biggest thing I'd raced prior to that day was a sprint car that weighed about fourteen hundred pounds. Stockcars weigh thirty-four hundred pounds. This was old-fashioned racing with big machines that had big rumbling engines and lots of metal.

This was also the first time I'd driven on a track with such high banking. In sprint cars and midgets, banking was non-existent. Rockingham has twenty-three degrees of banking in turns one and two, and twenty-five degrees in turns three and four. Driving into the corners with that much banking was the smoothest, best-feeling ride I'd ever taken. After turning a few laps, I was home. I was nineteen years old, and I knew what I wanted to do with my career.

I sped (literally) back to Pinehurst that night and burst into the hotel room. "Mom," I said. "I've found it. This is it. This is what I want to do for the rest of my life. This is it."

"Calm down, Jeff," she said. "So, you had a good day."

"Mom, this is great." I was pacing the room, waving my arms. "I love it. This is where I belong. I want to do this. We've got to call John."

"Hold on. I understand that you like this, but it's your first day. Let's give it a day or two and see how you feel before we bring John in."

I knew how I felt, but I understood that she was trying to keep me levelheaded. Mom and John were always good about that. I'd get revved up about something and start talking fast and loud and waving my arms, and they would step in and calm things down, always speaking softly and slowly, and making sure I was keeping my emotions in check. I can't think of a better trait for the parents of a racecar driver. If I'd been a football player or a track star, maybe a fiery pregame speech would have worked, but the last thing a racecar driver needs is somebody in his face getting him hyped up. There's plenty of adrenaline surging through you when you press the throttle. What you need from a coach (or a parent) is calm, focused, thoughtful advice.

The second day of the school, Buck introduced me to Hugh Connerty. Hugh owned the car we were driving. I later learned that just as Larry had worked out a deal with Buck, Buck had worked out a deal with Hugh. Hugh provided Buck with the car for the school, as long as Hugh could bring his real racecar out and turn a few laps at the track Buck had leased. Buck must have seen something in me, because he told Hugh he needed to come out and have a look and let me get into his racecar.

I couldn't wait to get into Hugh's car. The school car was fine, but it had a right seat and wasn't a car you would actually race. Hugh's racecar was ready for the Busch series. I thanked Hugh for the opportunity, then ran the best laps of the week. I later learned that my lap times were better than any Hugh had ever run in that car. After four laps, I came in and talked through what I was feeling with Hugh and Buck, and I told them how I thought we could make the car go faster. They both stared at me for a second. Then Hugh said the words that will forever ring in my ears.

"So," he said, "would you like to drive four or five Busch Grand National races for me if I can put a deal together?"

The only comparable analogy I can come up with would be if the director of NASA approached a promising young airline pilot and said, "So, would you like to pilot the space shuttle?" This was a one-in-a-million shot, but here I was being offered the opportunity of a lifetime. My heart rate jumped about a dozen beats a minute, and I tried my best not to let my voice crack. "Are you serious?" I said.

"You bet I am," Hugh said.

"Wow, that's great." I thanked Hugh a dozen times before realizing that I would have to clear this with my dad.

I was bouncing off the walls when I got back to the hotel. Mom and I called John immediately. "Okay, okay," he said. "I understand you're excited. This would be a great opportunity—"

"No, it would be the opportunity of a lifetime," I said.

"I understand that. But let's see what he comes back with. You know there are a lot of big talkers out there. If this guy can put up the goods, we'll see what happens."

I knew what John was saying. He was trying to protect me, and of course he was right. We didn't know much about Hugh; he might pull something together, and he might not.

The final day of the school, I convinced my mom to come out and ride a few laps with me in the right seat of the school's car. This was the first car I'd ever raced that had room for more than one person, and Hugh had installed a passenger seat in one of the test cars. I saw Mom's eyes go wide when they pulled the harness on her five-point seat belt and drew her spine flush against the seat. "This might be a mistake," she said.

"Nah," I said. "You'll be fine."

"I'm not sure I'm going to like this."

"You'll love it."

"Okay, just go slow."

I figure we were tracking at about 150 miles an hour when we entered turn three.

I couldn't hear her, but I could tell from the hand motions and the movement of her mouth that Mom wasn't having a good time. "Oh, God, Jeff, slow down! Slooooowwwwww down!" she later admitted to screaming. When we got out, she said, "What do you think you were doing going that fast with me in the car?"

"Mom, that was as slow as the car would go."

She knew right then and there that I had found my calling.

— — — — —

If Hugh had been some guy off the street, we probably wouldn't have taken his offer seriously. There are lots of well-intentioned people who want to put racing deals together, but who don't have the means to do it. One of the things Hugh had going for him was a family connection. His father-in-law was Leo Jackson, a big-time Winston Cup car owner who owned the car driven by Harry Gant.

I'm not sure how or even if Leo's connections helped, but Hugh did, indeed, put a three-race deal together. Outback Steakhouse was our sponsor. Our first test came in September of 1990 in Charlotte. This was a two-week testing period for Busch and Cup cars before the fall Charlotte race, and it would be my first test in a stockcar under anything resembling race conditions. Before the test, Hugh was scrambling to assemble the other pieces needed to field a race team. As I look back on it now, it's amazing we were able to race given how quickly everything was thrown together. At the time I didn't know any different. All I knew was I was going NASCAR racing.

One of the ways in which Hugh's family connection worked to our benefit was in bringing on personnel. Andy Petree, who is now a car owner, but who was Harry Gant's crew chief at the time, called a friend from New Jersey whom he'd met in the IROC series.

"There's a pretty good opportunity here," Andy said to Ray Evernham.

Ray was a show-me guy, just like my dad. In fact, their personalities were so similar it was scary at times. Ray listened and asked a few questions. Then he decided to make a trip down to Charlotte to meet me.

We hit it off right away, or at least I thought we did. In just a few minutes of speaking with Ray I had a great feeling about him. He reminded me of my dad, with different experiences and perspectives, but with the same drive and focus. I thought we had an instant chemistry.

I thought Ray felt the same way. Later I read how he described that first meeting. "The very first time I saw Jeff, he looked about fourteen or fifteen years old," Ray would say years later. "His mother was with him, and he had a briefcase in one hand. He called me Mr. Evernham. He was trying to grow a mustache, not very successfully, and when he opened his briefcase, he had a video game, a cell phone, and racing magazine in it. I asked myself, 'What am I getting myself into?' "

Three

Busch, Bill, and the Boy Who Didn't Bust His Butt

7 wasn't as immediately successful in NASCAR as many people think. I qualified second (outside front row) for my first race, which caught a lot of people's attention, but I crashed twenty-three laps into the race. The remaining two races with Hugh Connerty in late 1990 were uneventful at best. We didn't qualify and failed to make the race in Martinsville, Virginia. It wasn't outstanding by a long shot. Hugh worked his tail off trying to put another deal together for 1991, but as so often happens in our sport, he couldn't put the hundreds of pieces together to field a team.

It's unfortunate that Hugh couldn't pull something together. I owe him a lot and have no doubt I would have driven for him if he could have put a sponsor and some financing together. As history stands, he gave me the opportunity of a lifetime. He also arranged my introduction to Ray Evernham.

Just like any transition, it took a while for me to get the hang of Busch Grand National racing. The fundamentals of the sport were the same, but the transition from a fourteen-hundred-pound, seven-hundred-horsepower sprint car to a thirty-four-hundred-pound, six-hundred-horsepower Busch car is big. This was the first car I'd ever driven where I was enclosed in a cockpit. Sure, the driver's window is open (covered by netting), but in midgets and sprinters I was fully exposed with only a roll cage surrounding me. The wheelbases are different, the balance is different, and the aerodynamics are different. There were times in sprint car, midget, and particularly in dirt car racing where I expected the rear end of the car to get loose in every turn. The rear wheels slid out from under you, and you oversteered to get the car back on line, sort of a controlled skid. When a Busch car gets away from you, you're probably going into the wall.

I had also never driven in a league where rubbing was part of the strategy. In open-wheel racing there are no fenders. If you rub another driver, it's usually wheel to wheel, which often leads to a spectacular crash. Busch and Cup cars have fenders, and as the old NASCAR garage adage goes, "Rubbing is racing." Driving with forty-two other cars on the track was also something I had to get used to. Not only were the cars bigger, there were more of them out on the track running closer together and occasionally getting into each other.

Sure, I'd driven the car pretty well at Buck Baker's school, and I'd tested fairly well in Charlotte, but testing and qualifying is as different from racing as jogging through your neighborhood is from running in the Boston Marathon. I'm glad I had those initial races in 1990 to get the feel for weaving through traffic, trading paint with a few of my fellow drivers, and learning how a bigger, heavier car handled in the traffic and changing conditions of a race.

When the 1990 season ended, I was afraid my dreams were over. Hugh didn't have a sponsor, which meant I didn't have a ride. That's when my dad started working the phones. I hadn't won in those first three Busch starts, but I'd shown potential. People in the garage were aware of who I was, and what I wanted to do. Now we needed to find another owner who would take a chance on a not-quite-twenty-year-old kid who had all of three months' experience behind the wheel of a stockcar.

My break came when I got a call from a man named Lee Morse from Ford. Lee got straight to the point: "If you're interested, I might have a ride for you."

"You bet I'm interested," I said.

"Do you know the Carolina Ford Dealers' car owned by Bill Davis?"

"Sure I do. Mark Martin drives that car."

"Mark's leaving to own his own team. That ride's available," Lee said.

One meeting, a few phone calls, and a promise or two later, Bill and his wife, Gail, were on a plane to Indianapolis. Mom and John met them at the airport and took them to central Indiana's famous Frank & Mary's catfish restaurant, where the subject quickly turned to me driving Bill's car.

"What sort of salary would Jeff be looking for as a rookie driver?" Bill asked.

"No salary," John said.

Bill almost choked on his hush puppy. "What do you mean?" he finally asked.

"I mean Jeff doesn't want a salary to drive your car."

"What, is he going to drive for free?"

"No," John said. "We want a percentage of the car."

Bill stammered and shook his head. "No, he has to have a salary."

"Why? Why would you want to pay Jeff Gordon a big salary when you don't have to?"

Bill was listening.

"Look, we've always driven for a percentage of the car. We'll pay our own travel expenses. Then we'll take fifty percent of what the car makes. If the car makes money, Jeff makes money. If the car doesn't make money, Jeff doesn't make money."

John felt that this arrangement sold Bill Davis on me as his driver. At any moment, hundreds of guys are looking to break into NASCAR. Bill could have picked someone from the ASA or

ARCA series. These had been the farm clubs for Busch drivers for years. There was no reason for him to take a chance with a guy who'd been an open-wheel driver. Within a couple of days, I had an eleven-page contract to drive Bill Davis's Carolina Ford Dealers car in the 1991 Busch Grand National series.

— — — —

Things didn't go as well as I'd hoped at first. I failed to qualify for the field in the first race of the year, the Goody's 300 at Daytona International Speedway. That was my first racing experience at the legendary track, and I was angry that the car wasn't up to speed. The only other time I'd seen the superspeedway at Daytona was when John and I were traveling between Jacksonville and Tampa during All-Star Speedweeks. I don't think I'd ever seen a lap of the Daytona 500. Growing up in Indiana, the Indy 500 was my Super Bowl, and the only race I watched with any regularity. The other fifty-one weekends a year I was racing, so I didn't have time to watch other drivers, but I knew the history of the track and the significance of winning there. That made my poor showing even more depressing.

I improved a little in the next few weeks, but not as much as I'd hoped. We qualified twenty-seventh in Richmond the week after Daytona, and finished seventeenth, four laps behind the leader. I had a good qualifying run at Rockingham with the fourth-fastest time, but we finished nine laps back. In Martinsville, I qualified thirtieth and worked my up to fourteenth, a respectable showing, but still nothing that made headlines. We qualified fourth in Volusia, Florida, and in Hickory, North Carolina, we qualified second and finished fifteenth. These weren't world-beating statistics, but I was making steady progress each week. We were getting faster, and I was getting accustomed to being in a heavier car.

When we finished second at the Nestlé 200 in April, I really thought we had it all together. My goals for the 1991 season were to win a race, and take Rookie of the Year honors. When we finished eighth in the final race of the year in Martinsville (the Winston Classic), I had accomplished one out of two. I completed the year with five top-five finishes (including three runner-ups). I won one pole and completed 5,856 laps out of a possible 6,463. The car earned $111,608, and I accumulated 2,198 points, enough to barely squeak by David Green for Rookie of the Year. Only twelve points separated David and me at the end of the year, making it the closest Rookie of the Year race in recent history.

Unfortunately, I didn't win any races. I would have to wait another year for that milestone. I would also renew an old acquaintance, one that would prove invaluable to my future in racing.

— — — —

Ray Evernham wasn't my crew chief that first season. He had gone to work for Alan Kulwicki after the Hugh Connerty deal fell through. But at Daytona in 1992, our paths crossed again. After practice one afternoon I saw Ray leaving the track with his briefcase in hand. It wasn't time to leave, and I knew Ray wasn't calling it quits early. As we passed I said, "What's up?"

"Oh, I just quit," he said.

"You what?"

"Yeah. I've had it. Can't communicate with those guys, so I'm going home."

"Wait a minute. I want to hire you over at our place." Of course I was in no position to offer Ray a job, so I had a lot of selling to do. After a couple of intense conversations with Bill, Ray joined our team for the 1992 season.

My parents also liked Ray and thought he was good for me. Even though I was twenty years old and living on my own in Charlotte by the winter of 1991, my mom and dad continued to play a key role in my career. Like most twenty-year-olds, I didn't realize how much advice I needed, but my mom and dad struck a good balance between guiding me and getting out of my way so I could make decisions (good and bad) on my own. What they didn't have to tell me was how much they liked Ray Evernham. Ray and John were so much alike it didn't shock anyone when they became good friends. Plus, Ray's age—older than me, but younger than John—was perfect. He wasn't a father figure, but he sure could have passed as an uncle.

When Ray took over as crew chief in 1992, it was like coming home. Ray and I had chemistry. I could tell him the car was a little loose on drive-off and he'd know the degree of the problem by the inflection in my voice. He also wouldn't hesitate to get after me when I needed it. We respected each other, which meant we could be open and honest with each other, even in the heat of a race. I took Ray's words to heart because I knew he was looking out for my interests and the interests of the team.

I remember calling my mom one night after a practice session and saying, "You know, I never thought I'd meet somebody as dedicated and focused as John, but I have in Ray."

Mom agreed. Years later she would say, "Jeff was young at

the time, and he needed the sort of leadership and guidance he'd gotten from John, only not from John. We found that person in Ray."

We started 1992 with a new sponsor (Baby Ruth), a new crew chief, and a new outlook. I wanted to do more than win a race; I wanted to win the championship. With the team we had assembled, I thought we had a fighting chance.

Our luck in Daytona wasn't much better the second time around. I again failed to qualify in the Goody's 300, but was able to get into the race on a provisional start (which meant I started dead last out of forty-four cars). Throughout the day I worked my way up through the pack before blowing an engine on lap 102 of 120. We finished twenty-third. A week later in Rockingham, we won our first pole of the year and led twenty-two laps before falling back and finishing in ninth place.

Two races in, we could feel a difference. Ray was a natural leader. He had the command presence of a field general, and the motivating skills of a championship football coach. The crew had more of a spring in their steps when Ray was around. There wasn't a soul on our team who wouldn't work all night if Ray said that was what it took. Ray wouldn't ask anybody to do anything he wasn't ready, willing, and able to do himself, and nobody in the shop outworked him.

We won three poles in a row and contended every week, finishing ninth and sixth in weeks two and three. In the fourth race of the year we won the pole again, this time in the Atlanta 300, the first Busch race ever run at Atlanta Motor Speedway. The track was as fast as ever, and I was determined to push that car as hard as I could. I'd been racing stockcars in the Busch series for the better part of seventeen months, and we hadn't had a single victory. We had good cars, and we were having great runs; we just couldn't take that one last step. I figured this was our week. The finishes were nice, but I wasn't out there for top tens. I thought we were ready for Victory Lane.

That day in Atlanta, I led 103 of 197 laps. On the last lap I almost lost the darned thing because I was so choked up I had a hard time driving the car. "One to go," I heard Ray say over the headset. "Bring it on in." Those were the first time he'd uttered those words during a winning effort. I wanted to sear them into my brain along with the images of thousands of fans on their feet as I crossed the finish line.

This was what it was all about. This was why I'd come to NASCAR.

That day would prove to be prophetic in a number of ways. Not only was it my first win in a NASCAR series, it was my first victory with Ray Evernham calling the shots from the pits. For the first time since my dad and I had traveled the sprint car circuit, I felt like I had a crew chief I could win with every week.

– – – – –

What I didn't know at the time and wouldn't know for many months was the new fan I picked up that afternoon in Atlanta. Rick Hendrick, one of the premier car owners on the Winston Cup circuit and a guy who had put cars under such world-class drivers as Darrell Waltrip, Benny Parsons, Ricky Rudd, and Tim Richmond, was at the track that day almost by accident. As Rick tells the story, "I did everything that day that I never do. I wasn't normally at the track during the Busch race because I didn't have a Busch car at the time. I was walking to one of our sponsors' suites in the infield—Atlanta is one of the only tracks that has an infield personnel tunnel—and I wasn't even watching because I didn't even know who was in the race. But as I walked out of the tunnel, I turned around and saw this car coming around turn four. I saw the haze coming off the tires that happens when the car's loose.

"Atlanta is a fast track, so I assumed he was going to get out of the throttle. The car wiggled a little bit, but he kept pressing it through the turn. I turned to my friends and said, 'Let's watch this guy a minute. He's about to bust his butt.' But he never did. We watched him run another ten laps and he did the same thing every time. I asked one of my guys, 'Who is that?' And he said, 'That's Jeff Gordon.'

"All that day and the next day that image kept creeping into my brain. I couldn't get rid of it. I came back to the office in Charlotte and said to the manager of my motorsports division, 'I watched this kid, Gordon, and I hear he's only nineteen.' My manager said, 'Yeah, it's a shame he's got a contract.'

"A fellow named Andy Graves who worked for me just happened to be in the room at the time and said, 'He doesn't have a contract. I live with him. I'm his roommate. He has a one-year deal, and that's it.' When the kid said that, I figured this was one of those things that was just meant to be."

Andy was right. The contract I had with Bill Davis and Ford was year to year. If Bill thought things weren't working out, he could give me notice and send me packing, and if I found another opportunity, especially in Winston Cup, I could give notice and move to another team. That wasn't my plan, though. Bill was working on a Winston Cup sponsorship for the following year, and if he came through, I would happily drive for him. But Ray and I knew that if Bill didn't have something in place by May, we wouldn't have the time or the resources to go Cup racing with him the following year.

Not long after that race in Atlanta, Andy came home and said, "Hey, man, Rick Hendrick wants you to call him."

"Get out of here," I said. "Rick Hendrick does not want me calling him."

"No, man, I'm serious. Rick told me to tell you to call him. He saw you in Atlanta. I think he wants to talk to you about a ride."

"You're messing with me, Andy."

"Whatever. I've passed along the message."

I went about my business as if that conversation had never taken place.

The week after our win in Atlanta we qualified twenty-seventh in the Miller 500 at Martinsville and worked our way up to finish sixth. Five weeks into the season, and we had four top tens and a win. We blew an engine the next week at Darlington, but a week later we were right back in the hunt in Bristol with a fifth-place finish from the outside pole.

We were on a roll. It was like that first victory had broken the dam. We were running fast and strong every week. I've been asked a lot of times over the years to explain how an auto racing team gets on a run. When a hitter in baseball gets on a streak, the ball looks like a slow-moving grapefruit as it's coming toward the plate. When a golfer gets on a roll, the hole looks like a crater and his swing feels automatic. Nothing can go wrong. But every week we race on different tracks, in different conditions, with different cars. So if the machines are different, the track is different, and the conditions are different, what is it that allows a race team to get on a roll?

If I had to sum it up in two words, they would be *confidence* and *chemistry.* That second year of Busch racing, and in several of the seasons I've had in Winston Cup, we showed up knowing we had a good chance at winning. We believed in ourselves and we let our actions speak for us.

On a sunny Saturday in May we showed the world what kind of competitors we were. It happened at the Charlotte Motor Speedway in the Champion 300, the first of two Busch races in Charlotte that year. I had posted two more top tens in the four weeks prior to that race, and during the first three months of the season it seemed that in any race where we didn't blow an engine or have mechanical trouble, we were contending on the final laps. But we needed another win, and Charlotte was the best place to do it.

At lap 163 I knew we had a winning car, but I'd been battling Mark Martin all day. Mark was one of the first drivers I'd met when I'd got into Busch racing, because he was the guy who had driven the Carolina Ford Dealers car before me. What struck me about him was that he was a quiet, unassuming, cordial fellow in the garage, and as fierce a competitor on the track as I had ever seen. In one of my first Busch races I remember seeing Mark drive so hard into a corner that the car almost got sideways on him. At that time I thought, "This guy's got heart." I also remember thinking that anybody who thought Mark Martin's quiet personality was a sign that he was soft was in for a shock when meeting him on the track.

Lap traffic was thick, which made it almost impossible to pass. I saw my chance in turn four. Dick Trickle hadn't come in during a green-flag pit stop, so he had the lead, but he was running into lap traffic. When he gave a lapped car a wide berth, going high and wide through the center of the turn, I knew I had him. The gap between Dick's front left fender and the right rear fender of the lapped car was just enough for me to squeeze through. I probably had an inch or two on either side, but a gap was a gap. Sometimes you have to be superaggressive if you're going to win. This was one of those times.

I felt a wiggle as my car nudged Dick's rear fender. Then I saw and heard him back out of the throttle. I knew I had him. By the time we crossed the start-finish line, I was in the lead by a full car-length over Mark Martin, who had followed me through the same hole. It was a lead I wouldn't relinquish the rest of the afternoon.

"That's what I'm talking about!" I heard Ray say over the radio. "Great move. You got it. Now, bring it on in."

Afterward, I was asked about that final pass. I looked right into the camera and said, "I had a lot of close calls out there, and that was one of them."

If there were any questions in the Busch garages about our intentions, I think we answered them that afternoon.

– – – – –

There were still some unanswered questions in the offices at Hendrick Motorsports, however. The most pressing one from Rick was "Why the heck hasn't Jeff Gordon called me?" Andy was on the receiving end of this one, and he was running out of excuses for me. The son of a tobacco-farming father and a bank-teller mother, Rick started with a lone Chevrolet dealership and built it into one of the largest retail automobile empires in the world. He is also one of the people who brought the NBA to his hometown, putting a deal together to create the Charlotte Hornets, and he has one of the most successful motorsports franchises in racing. I didn't think he was really interested in me.

Andy was caught in the middle. I was doing what Bill Davis had hired me to do: drive the car as fast and hard as I could and put us in contention for a championship, while my roommate was fielding questions from his boss. I wasn't trying to be rude; I just wasn't sure Rick really wanted to talk with me, and even if he did, I wasn't sure what we would talk about. Bill had been the owner who had given me a chance, and he was the guy I was loyal to in 1992. We were having a good run (six more top-five finishes, including another win at the fall race in Charlotte) and I didn't need any distractions. If we won, I figured I'd have lots of people wanting to talk to me. If we didn't, people would say, "Jeff who?"

What I didn't understand was the situation my roommate was in. Rick was serious, and every time he would ask Andy about me, Andy would tap-dance as fast as he could. Finally, Andy pulled a desperation move. He was close to my family, having lived with us for a while in Pittsboro. So he picked up the phone and called my dad.

"Look," Andy said. "I know it's not your problem, and Jeff's a grown man, but Rick Hendrick wants Jeff to call him, and I can't get Jeff to believe me. He won't call Rick back."

John thanked Andy and talked the situation over with Mom. "I know Jeff's going to be mad at me, but I'm going to call Rick Hendrick," John said.

I wasn't mad. I just wasn't sure Rick was truly interested in me, and I felt obligated to give Bill until May to put a Winston Cup deal together. When John called me, he said, "Jeff, Rick is talking about putting you in a Cup car next year. Now, you owe it to yourself to at least call the man."

John was right. It was now May, and while Bill was still calling potential sponsors, things weren't looking promising. Rick, on the other hand, had the resources to field a team without a sponsor for a season if he wanted to. He was also one of the most creative thinkers in our sport. He was one of the first owners to run a multiple-team operation at a time when such a thing was considered insane. It was hard enough to focus on one team; how could you be successful with two or more cars? And what would you do when teammates competed against each other?

These were the issues Rick had successfully worked through. As he explains it, "I've always tried new stuff. I've had multiple car dealerships and seen the benefits there, so I knew the management style would work in motorsports. The one thing I learned from owning so many franchises is that you always have one star in every location. One dealership might have a better parts department, and another might have a better sales and service department. What you try to do is bring them all up to the same level in every area so you have a benchmark. Everybody gets better because you've got stars in each area setting examples. That philosophy works in my businesses. I saw no reason why it wouldn't work with my race teams."

I liked this concept. I knew I could drive a racecar, and Ray could put the best team on the track, but without the best engines, best chassis, best engineers, best infrastructure, and best financial support, we would always be playing catch-up to somebody. Rick could provide us with that "baseline" support. He could give us the best cars and best motors, and he was confident enough to let Ray and I do our own thing from there. He would give us the tools and provide advice and support.

The more I listened, the more I liked what I heard.

Rick was willing to take a chance on me. As he put it, "Nobody had ever tried to run a multicar deal with a kid that age. Usually you've got a team and a sponsor lined up first, and the driver is one of the final components. I did exactly the opposite. I offered Jeff a job without having a sponsor, a team, or even a car for him. A lot of folks thought I was nuts, but I knew he had what it took. He had the looks, the personality, the skills, and Bickford had groomed him in a way that was far beyond his years. I figured I could get this incredible talent at a young age and mold him into a winning system. It was like getting a thoroughbred before anybody knows anything about him."

Not having a sponsor in place might have scared some guys off, but I realized that Rick was a man of his word, as well as a man with the financial means to go racing with or without a sponsor for while. That Rick didn't have a team or a crew chief in place made pitching the idea of bringing Ray along a lot easier.

I was still a little torn. Bill Davis had been good to me. He'd given me an opportunity to break into our sport. But I realized that if I was going to win a lot of championships, I had to align myself with the best. Rick was that guy. He loved winning as much as I did, and I loved it more than food and water. Plus, Rick had something to prove. No multicar owner had ever won a championship. Rick had come close many times, but he hadn't been able to finish on top with two cars on the track. If I proved a winner, Rick would make sure I had every resource I needed. From a business standpoint, and for my own future, the decision was easy. I knew I couldn't say no.

NASCAR is a big business and a huge sport, but it's also a small, tight-knit community. We're like the traveling circus: every week our caravans roll into town and we set up for a weekend show. The drivers, crews, support staff, officials, and reporters travel together, eat together, lodge together, and know everything there is to know about everybody else's business. It didn't take long for word of my negotiations with Rick Hendrick to filter through the garages.

The folks at Ford almost had a collective coronary. Rick was a Chevy guy, and while Ford hadn't thought highly enough of me to offer a long-term contract, when they heard I might go Cup racing in a Chevrolet, they pulled out all the stops. The guys from Ford called and made some threatening noises, but I told them, "Hey, if you'd locked me into a contract, we wouldn't be having these discussions. I will honor my commitment to you and to Bill, and anything that happens in the future will be done in accordance with the contracts I have in place."

The most interesting call came from Jack Roush, a famous race team owner. Jack fielded a Ford team and made a call to my dad about the possibility of me moving to Roush Racing. When John mentioned that I wanted to bring Ray with me, Jack interrupted, "My drivers don't hire my crew chiefs. I hire my crew chiefs."

That effectively ended the discussion.

One week and several hundred faxes later, I signed a contract with Hendrick Motorsports for the 1993 season.

My mom wasn't thrilled, but I couldn't have been happier my first day behind the wheel of a quarter midget in 1977.

Previous page: While other kids my age were playing Little League baseball, I spent my weekends at the track.

An early victory lap in a quarter midget.

Once I got used to 700-horsepower sprint cars, I loved them. Here I am setting a track record in a sprinter at the Lawrenceburg Speedway in Indiana.

The Diet Pepsi Midget, owned by Rollie Helmling, gave me my first exposure to a national sponsor.

My first two seasons in NASCAR I drove a Ford owned by Bill Davis in the Busch Grand National series. Our second year, Baby Ruth was the primary sponsor.

Left: A sprint car victory in Bloomington, Indiana.

Following page: I've been driving cars for most of my life, but the intensity I feel when I put on that race helmet hasn't changed one bit. *CIA Stock Photo*

– – – – –

The hard part came the next day. Bill Davis and I flew to Minneapolis to meet with executives from Target department stores concerning a possible sponsorship. We went through the presentation, but my stomach was in knots. I had to break the news to Bill, but I didn't want to do it before the sponsor presentation. He needed to be on his game, and I wanted him to get the sponsor. What I had to tell him would certainly distract him. On the flight back to Charlotte, I told Bill that I would be leaving at the end of the season and moving to Winston Cup with Rick Hendrick.

Bill didn't take it well. He felt slighted, and I can't say I blame him. He was doing the best he could to put a sponsorship deal together so we could go Cup racing in 1993, but he didn't have any commitments. On the other hand, Rick didn't have a sponsor, either, but in his case, he didn't care. He was willing to offer me a generous contract and allow me to bring my own crew chief before he had a sponsor, a team, or a space carved out in his shop for us to work. I tried to explain my decision to Bill, but I wasn't very successful. From a business point of view it was a no-brainer. But Bill didn't see it as a business decision; he took it as a personal slight.

The next few weeks were eye-opening. I know NASCAR fans are loyal to their brands, particularly cars, but I wasn't prepared for the venomous reaction I got when word got out about my Chevy deal. Local papers ran stories about my lack of loyalty to Bill Davis, and how I'd hung a good man out to dry. Nothing could have been further from the truth. If Bill had come to me with a sponsor and a reasonable plan to go Winston Cup racing,

I would have stayed. But by the time we flew to Minneapolis to meet with the Target people, it was already too late for us to put together a competitive Cup team.

Others didn't see it that way. Ford's director of special operations, a guy named Michael Kranefuss, summed up the opinion of most pundits when he asked, "Why would a young kid who has won over six hundred races be so blind and a team up with somebody who couldn't make a two-car team work and now wants to make a three-car team?" I even got letters from Bill Davis's shop that were, um, less than flattering.

As I told anybody who asked at the time, "Bill Davis and Ford treated me well and gave me a lot of opportunities. But they didn't make me the driver that I am. If Bill had put a deal together, I would probably have stayed."

After a week of bad press and negative buzz in Charlotte, I finally called my dad and said, "You need to come down here. This is getting out of control."

John came down and spent a few days with me, which was a blessing. He didn't have any profound insight into why people behaved the way they did, but I felt better having him around. After a couple of weeks, the dust settled and I was no longer headline news. This was my first experience with how passionate stockcar fans can be, and I certainly learned a lot from it.

Unfortunately, Bill Davis Racing remained pretty chilly the rest of the year. I drove Bill's car as hard as I could every week and remained in the hunt for the championship right up until the final few weeks of the season. I won a late-season event in Bill's car and did everything I could to put a professional face on the situation. But Bill was hurt, and he showed it. At the final race of the year in Hickory, we started on the outside pole and finished eleventh. That was the end of my professional relationship with Bill Davis.

I wish it could have ended on a better note. I understood Bill's feelings, and I wish he had understood mine. We were going Cup racing with a chance of winning. That had to be my primary focus.

Four

Car and Driver

7 t's the age-old question in racing: How much of a winning performance can be attributed to the car, and how much credit goes to the driver? I've heard some drivers try to assign percentages—*80 percent car/20 percent driver, 50/50, 60/40 driver over car*—but I've avoided that sort of analysis. To try to separate car, team, and driver and then decide who contributes most is like saying Joe Montana was responsible for half or three-quarters of the San Francisco 49ers' wins, and the other forty-four players only account for one-quarter, or that Derek Jeter accounts for eighty of the Yankees' wins in any given season. Montana wouldn't have lasted one down without the other ten players on offense, and he couldn't have scored enough points if the Niners fielded a JV defensive squad. Jeter might bat .900 for the season, but without good pitching, good defense, and a full complement of professionals around him, the Yankees wouldn't win a game.

Racing is the same way. A good driver is important; a good car is important; a good crew chief is important; and a competent and motivated crew is important. This is a team sport where car, driver, and crew are linked. A team might have the most skilled driver in history, but without a good racecar he's going to run in the back of the pack. The same team might have a great racecar, but if the driver is little too high-strung or inexperienced, they're going to be hauling a wrecked chassis back to the garage. Then, there's the crew. If you have a great car and a great driver, but you spend forty-five seconds in the pits while the teams around you are in and out in between fourteen and sixteen seconds, you're never going to contend. All the pieces have to come together, and all the players have to gel to take the checkered flag on Sunday.

That people ask about the role of driver and car, and arguments ensue over man versus machine, is odd. Folks might argue over whether Shaquille O'Neal and Kobe Bryant are the most dominant players in the NBA, but nobody thinks the two of them could beat the Clippers in a game of two on five. Without other players, a coach, a front office, and a support staff, and without a great working chemistry between themselves, Shaq and Kobe would be great players stuck on a losing team. And nobody believes otherwise. So, why does the question of "Car or driver?" come up in racing?

I think NASCAR has a lot to do with it. NASCAR has gone out of its way to make this a driver's sport. Drivers are promoted as stars, and NASCAR institutes rules to bring the cars closer together in performance. Officials don't want Winston Cup to be about who has the best computer or best aerodynamics package. To attract new fans, NASCAR has decided to narrow the equipment gap, so it can make the Winston Cup a driver's championship.

That strategy has paid off. NASCAR has experienced phenomenal growth in the past decade. It's second only to the NFL in terms of American viewers and fans. The downside to this success comes when new fans conclude that drivers are 50, 60, 70, or 80 percent of the team. We are only as good as the men and the car around us, and they are only as good as the man behind the wheel. You cannot separate one from the other.

– – – – –

I was thrilled when Bill Davis hired Ray Evernham as my crew chief in 1991 because I knew Ray was a winner, and I needed somebody like him leading the crew. Rick Hendrick also had a burning desire to win, and I knew he and Ray shared similar values. With those two working side by side I knew there would never be a day when I climbed into inferior equipment, or when our team showed up at the track less than fully prepared.

At the time I wished most of the race world could have seen my side. In addition to catching flack from Ford fans for jumping to a Chevrolet team, I had to listen to an endless parade of experts who thought I had lost my last marble for signing with an owner who already had two Winston Cup cars. With Rick, I had two teammates: Ricky Rudd and Ken Schrader. I liked both of those guys and looked forward to learning from their Cup experience. Ken had come to NASCAR from open-wheel racing, so I looked forward to picking his brain and seeing if his experiences were similar to mine. But the question was still out there: If Rick couldn't win a championship with two cars, why did we think he could do it with three? This was during a time when running multiple cars out of one shop was a new idea. Some of Rick's former drivers—Darrell Waltrip among them—had left the multicar concept to become driver-owners. No owner with more than one car under his roof had ever won a championship. Smaller, not bigger, seemed to be the way the sport was heading.

So, why would a young driver like me become the third wheel in an operation that wasn't getting the job done with two cars? One trip to Hendrick Motorsports answered that question for me. Today, the compound, a couple of miles from the Lowe's Motor Speedway in Charlotte, has twelve buildings totaling four hundred thousand covered and heated square feet where more than four hundred people work in motorsports. Rick has more engineers, fabricators, and race-engine experts than anyone else in the business. I knew from my first day at Hendrick Motorsports that this operation was on the cutting edge of racing. I also saw something in Rick: a fire in his eyes. This guy was a winner, even if his teams hadn't come through for him yet. After an afternoon with Rick, my first thought wasn't "How am I going to win?" it was "How can anybody else compete against this?"

I also think a lot of the multicar grumbling stemmed from professional jealousy. Prior to my signing with Rick, nobody had ever run three teams, not because they didn't think it was possible, but because most owners didn't have the resources. Most were stretched thin with two teams; a third car was unthinkable. As a result, a lot of people accused Rick of violating an understanding among owners against running three-car teams. If there was such an agreement, it was in place to keep guys like Rick, who had the resources to put multiple teams out there, from gaining a competitive advantage.

Some people wondered out loud how two or three teammates would race against each other. Those who broached that subject didn't understand the competitive nature of racing. If it comes down to the last lap, I'm going to race my teammate just as hard as I would anybody else. I was brought up to race hard, but race clean, and that was what I would do for Rick. If anybody thought otherwise, they didn't know me very well.

Fortunately, in that first year I didn't have a lot of time to deal with those questions. Within a week of my last race for Bill

Davis, we unveiled the Dupont 24 Chevy Lumina at Rockingham Motor Speedway in front of a few hundred fans. The paint scheme was visually stunning, a bright, multicolored rainbow that was unlike anything else being run in the Winston Cup series. The first think I said was "Holy cow, that's bright!" It was certainly different. I thought it was a little loud to be honest, but then I realized that it would make a statement, which is what we wanted to do. It didn't matter to me how we painted the car; I couldn't wait to get behind the wheel.

— — — —

I got my chance in the final Winston Cup race of the 1992 season at Atlanta Motor Speedway. The Busch series had concluded before the final race of the Winston Cup season, and Rick didn't waste any time getting our team onto the track. With only one race left, we weren't contending for the championship, but we wanted to be competitive in this race. DuPont had taken a gamble with a rookie, and Rick wanted to give the company their money's worth. I was thrilled. Atlanta was a great track to make my debut and get some experience.

My adjustment from Busch to Winston Cup cars came quicker than I'd expected. Busch motors generate about six hundred horsepower, while Cup cars produce about seven hundred fifty horses. On the surface, you would assume Cup cars are quite a bit faster than Busch cars, but other factors were involved. Cup cars were a hundred pounds heavier than Busch cars at the time, and the wheelbase of Cup cars was five inches longer. I loved the added stability, and I immediately felt comfortable in the car. The only adjustment I had to make was how deep I drove the car into the corners. With the lighter weight and shorter wheelbase of the Busch cars, I could make a sharp entry into banked corners like the ones in Atlanta. The heavier, more powerful Winston Cup cars made it more difficult to drive in deep. I also had to adjust to the longer races of the Winston Cup series. More laps and more pit stops requires a different mind-set and a different approach, and it took a few races for me to adjust to that.

I loved it, especially given how quick a car we had in Atlanta. Unfortunately, I didn't do as well in the race as I did in practice. I started the race in the twenty-first spot. We worked our way through the pack, but on lap 160 the car got loose, I spun out, and we finished thirty-first for the day.

I didn't know it at the time, but a lot of the people and events of that day would come back around to play a role in my life. While I was thrilled to be out on the track in the Winston Cup series, our debut was overshadowed by the fact that 1992 was Richard Petty's last season as a driver, and the race in Atlanta was his final event behind the wheel. If there were 200,000 people at the track that day, 190,000 of them were there to see The King, which is how it should have been. Richard set a bar for our sport that will never be matched. Not only did he win two hundred Winston Cup races and seven championships, he established an unwritten code of conduct for those who came after him. Richard is a great champion, an ambassador of our sport, a tireless spokesman for the sponsors that support us, and above all, a gentleman. To have made my Winston Cup debut at his final race was a thrill.

Some of the reporters that week (who were looking for a story angle) asked if I thought of myself as the next-generation

Richard Petty. I told them, "I'd like to think that someday when people think of me, they would say just one one-hundredth of the nice things they say about Richard. Even that's probably too much to expect. I don't think anybody can be another Richard Petty. I think it's really neat to have your name mentioned with him, but let's be practical. Being put in the same category as The King puts a pretty big burden on your shoulders. I'm just trying to be Jeff Gordon."

Richard didn't have a good day in Atlanta, either. He was involved in an accident and finished thirty-fifth. He and his crew were done before we were, so they got a chance to hear the statements I made to the press.

Among those who heard me was Richard's crew chief, a quiet, confident, smiling twenty-eight-year-old named Robbie Loomis.

— — — — —

We won our first race out of the box in 1993. It was the Gatorade 125, the qualifier race at Daytona, a track where my history had been a little less than stellar. This was the first race of Speedweek, and we earned exactly zero points for the win, but when I came across that finish line, you'd have thought we'd just won our first championship. We were the first rookie team to win the 125 in thirty years, and I was the youngest winning driver (at age twenty-one) in the history of the event, a fact I put on display immediately after the win when I drove around lost for a few seconds because I didn't know how to get to Victory Lane. (We had a good laugh about that one.)

Seeing the checkered flag; seeing our team members hug

each other and raise their fists in the air in celebration; seeing other drivers and other crews giving us the thumbs-up—those were sights and sounds I would never forget, and feelings I wanted to experience again and again.

In the Daytona 500, I think we stunned the fans and the rest of the drivers by jumping up from our third-place qualifying position to lead the first lap. I didn't know it at the time, but no rookie had ever led the first lap at Daytona. It felt pretty good, and I was thrilled be up front. This was the biggest race of the year, and I was still learning. All I was looking for was a re-spectable finish. To lead the first lap, or any lap for that matter, was a special feeling.

A five-hundred-mile race is exhausting. Think of the last time you got in a tight situation on the interstate. You probably sat a little straighter in the seat, tightened your grip on the wheel, and put all your senses on high alert. When you got out of the situation, which probably happened in a minute or less, you realized how tense you had gotten. Now, imagine sustain-ing that level of intensity for five hundred miles at speeds ex-ceeding 190 miles per hour. That's what we go through every week. It is grueling.

Every rookie had to wear a rookie stripe on the rear fender for identification. I used the stripe as a motivator. I didn't want to be viewed as an inexperienced rookie, even though that's ex-actly what I was.

We ran strong all day, making the car better as track condi-tions changed and being smart and patient about how we picked our way through the field. If we'd led after a hundred laps, I would have been ecstatic. When I was running in second place behind Dale Earnhardt with only three laps to go, I was almost in shock. I couldn't believe how well we were running, especially with so few laps to go.

Dale Jarrett made a move to my inside, and I had a split second to make a decision. If I fell in behind D.J., I might overtake Earnhardt, but finish second to Jarrett. If I stayed behind Earnhardt, we might both overtake Jarrett and challenge each other for the title on the final lap. I went with the odds. I thought Dale Earnhardt was the best in the field at Daytona, even though he'd never won a Daytona 500, so I took my chances behind the black number 3. This wasn't one of those decisions I pondered. I made it in less than a second. It proved to be a mistake. I should have recognized that Earnhardt's car was going away from him on the closing laps, while Jarrett's car was getting stronger. Geoff Bodine fell in behind D.J. and both cars sped past me.

I finished fifth, an ending that had the NASCAR faithful buzzing. Our finish excited me, but I felt that my inexperience had cost us. There was nothing I could do about it, but I didn't like it.

— — — — —

It was one thing to catch everybody off guard at Daytona in the first race of the year, but I needed to follow it up. Fortunately we had good runs in Richmond, where we finished sixth, and had a fourth-place finish in Atlanta. Four races into the season, I had three top-ten finishes. Four weeks later, I had an eighth-place finish in Martinsville, Virginia, the shortest oval track on the NASCAR circuit and one where bumping and banging are part of the race. In Charlotte at the Coca-Cola 600, I posted my first runner-up finish after starting twenty-first, and three weeks later, I worked my way up from twenty-third to finish second in Michigan. I led three laps in Michigan and was running down the leader, Ricky Rudd, when we ran out of laps. This was when I realized that we were going to win some races. At that point, our confidence shot up. After that Michigan race I said to the media, "The car was awesome the last hundred laps, and I felt we really had a chance of winning the race. We just needed a little luck. I was running down Ricky. I think I could have made a winning move on him if I'd had another lap."

Some people took this the wrong way, and in hindsight I can understand why. I was the youngest driver in the field by a mile, and there I was saying things like I "really had a chance of winning the race." This sort of thing from a rookie took a lot of people by surprise, and not in a good way. I think I got a little arrogant in my rookie year. What I hadn't learned yet was just how quickly this sport can humble you. It was a lesson I would learn all too well in years to come.

At the time I was unaware of anybody rooting against me. We were cheered every week, and I saw our fan base growing with every stop. Suddenly, people were showing up at races wearing our shirts and hats, and carrying posters and pictures for me to sign. I'd had some fans here and there growing up, but there's a big difference in having two dozen gearheads at a sprint car track ask you for your autograph and having hundreds of people line up for a couple of hours in the hope that you'll sign their T-shirt (which also has your picture on it). The better we ran, the more demands were placed on my time, but I never lost sight of the ultimate goal. We raced hard every week and I felt sure we would break into the winner's circle in our first season. In hindsight, that was unrealistic.

As the season went along I discovered that the biggest difference between Winston Cup and the other series was parity. The best Busch drivers were almost as good as the best Cup drivers, but the gap between the top Busch team and thirtieth-best Busch team was substantial. In Winston Cup, the difference between the top team and the bottom team was minute. Every driver could drive. All the crew chiefs knew what they were doing. The crews were trained professionals, and there was only a fractional difference in the cars. This was a big change for me. By the latter half of the year I realized that I was going to lose a lot more than I was going to win at this level. I didn't have to like it, and I certainly didn't want to get used to it, but those were the facts of life.

We finished the year with four more top tens, and we won one pole at the fall race in Charlotte, but no victories. We finished fourteenth in points, and I won Rookie of the Year honors. By the time I stood on the stage at the Waldorf-Astoria in New York to accept the award, my life had changed. I was no longer the kid nobody knew. I was engaged to Miss Winston (the beauty queen who presented the trophies and checks to the winners), Brooke Sealey, and would marry her the following year. I wasn't Rick Hendrick's third wheel anymore, or the youngster nobody expected much from. I'd lost my rookie stripe, my anonymity, and the luxury of low expectations.

— — — — —

Ray and I talked a lot about winning, especially in the early stages of 1994 since neither of us had smelled victory in over a year. We tested a lot that year. With one full season under our belts, we knew what we liked and what we didn't in the setups for the various tracks. Testing in January was a way to further tweak what we'd already learned. It was a thankless, no-fun process, one you never looked forward to, but one you knew you had to go through to get better. Out in the primary car for four laps, then out in the backup car for four laps while changes were made to the primary, then repeat; this was how you refined your setups and got your speeds up at the various tracks. We liked what we saw in those early tests. Our team was as focused and driven as any I had ever seen. Now, all we needed was a win.

Ray and I talked a good deal about our first win, and when and how it might come. A win was always a win, and you would take one any way you could, but because we had run so well without a victory, we hoped our first win would come with a full complement of cars behind us.

I knew we were right on the cusp of doing something special, but we hadn't gotten there yet. Until we did, we were just a young team with a lot of promise. Ray was a little more patient (the gap in our ages probably had something to do with that), but he was also hungry. I could hear urgency in his voice. Posters went up on the shop floor—"The Team That Makes the Fewest Mistakes Will Get the Opportunity to Win," "The Disciplined Team Has to Be Beaten; It Refuses to Beat Itself," and my personal favorite, "The Hardest Workers Catch All the Breaks." At the beginning of the year Ray had posted a checklist, sort of a "things to do" list, in the garage. It read:

From Nobody to Upstart
From Upstart to Contender

From Contender to Winner
From Winner to Champion
From Champion to Dynasty

The first two boxes were checked, just like you'd check items off a grocery list. Ray wanted nothing more than to put a check in that third box.

— — — — —

We arrived at Daytona with fire in our eyes. Once again, we won an early Speedweek event, this time taking the Busch Clash, a special event featuring the pole winners from the previous season. When the 500 rolled around, we ran well again, but finished fourth after leading seven laps. Two weeks later we finished third in Richmond, and a week after that in Atlanta we worked our way up from eighteenth at the start of the race to eighth at the finish.

That Richmond race was one of our more frustrating weeks of the season. We had a great car. I had worked us up through the pack, and I was sure we had a chance to win. Then on lap 276, I came in for a scheduled pit stop. We changed four tires and filled the car with fuel. When the jack dropped and the left tires hit the ground, I punched the throttle. That was my cue to get out of the pits and back into the race. I didn't make it far. Before I got to the pit exit I could tell the car was wobbly. A second later, the left front fender dove for the ground like the car had been shot. Up ahead I saw my left front tire bouncing and rolling toward the track. We hadn't gotten the lugs tightened, and we were going nowhere on three wheels.

To their credit, the pit crew didn't hang their heads after the mistake. They sprinted out and got another tire on the car quickly enough to get me back out in ninth place. I finished the day in third place, but I couldn't help thinking about what could have been.

And on it went. We blew an engine in Darlington and got tangled up in a wreck in Bristol. At Talladega we had our worst qualifying run of the season, barely making the show with the fortieth-fastest car out of forty-three possible spots. But we worked out the kinks by race day and I was able to weave the car into the lead. Then with four laps to go, we got caught in another wreck and finished twenty-fourth. I started feeling like that kid in the comics with a black cloud following him. One thing was certain: we needed a break as badly as any team out there.

Four months into the season we were still searching for that break. The last week of May we finally got it less than two miles from our shop.

My mind-set when we race in Charlotte is different from in other weeks. For one thing, we aren't in our own little world out at the track; Charlotte is home for most of the drivers and all of the crew, so we all have friends and family in town, plus a quarter of a million visitors who are in town for the week. It's exciting, but there are added distractions. Just driving to the store for a gallon of milk is no small task. But sleeping at home and eating out of your own refrigerator makes life a little easier, as does having your shop within jogging distance of the track. Travel isn't an issue, which means you have one more day to get everything ready to race, and all your support staff is close by if you need them.

I knew we had a great car that week. During qualifying I was grinning from ear to ear before I got it through turn three, because I knew we'd won the pole. The setup was perfect. The car was as neutral (neither loose nor pushy) as any I'd had all year, and I felt like we were glued to the track as I drove it into the corners. We would start the race from the inside front row (called the pole, a holdover from the days when auto races were held on horse tracks where the tallest fence poll in the front stretch was the start-finish line). But we'd won poles before and hadn't won any races. We still had to put together a flawless performance.

The car ran great for most of the day. We were either leading or in the first five cars on the track for most of the race. When a caution came out with about a hundred laps to go, we had a great stop, but came out of the pits running third behind Rusty Wallace and Dale Jarrett. We raced in that order through lap 370 when everybody started worrying about fuel and tires. None of the leaders was going to make it the final thirty laps without another pit stop. The question was, would we all pit under green or was another caution in our future?

This is the gamble crew chiefs take every week. A racecar will only run so far on a set of tires before they get hot and wear out. All those things affect the way the car handles. If a car is tight or "pushes" in the turns, I'll call that in to the crew chief and we will evaluate the problem during the run. If the car is loose, we might decide to put on new tires with different air pressures in an attempt to tighten the car up or simply wait until our fuel level gets lower and the car tightens up as it gets lighter. Of course, the greatest tire strategy in the world doesn't matter if you run out of gas. At Charlotte that day, we knew we had to pit for both tires and fuel, and the crew chiefs had to break out their crystal balls and predict whether there would be another accident and caution flag in the final thirty laps of the race. If there was, the leaders could pit under yellow without worrying about giving up track position. If we pitted under green and a caution followed, we were in trouble.

Rusty was the first to come in. Dale was next. I came in right behind them, but with a different plan. Ray and I talked about it briefly, but not in enough detail to give away our strategy. NASCAR fans with scanners can listen in to conversations between the drivers and the crew chiefs, but other teams can listen in as well. When I pulled down pit road, Ray made the call that would change our day.

"Two tires," he said. "Right side only."

The other drivers were getting all four tires changed, meaning their stops would take about eighteen seconds. We were only changing the right-side tires (since we travel counterclockwise around the track, the right tires bear the heaviest loads in the turns). That decision got us in and out of the pits in just a shade over ten seconds. We left pit road with a 250-yard lead over Rusty Wallace.

Now the question was, could we hold it? Taking right tires only was risky. The left tires were hotter, more worn, and the air pressure was built up inside them. If the air pressures weren't perfect, it could make it a handful. Fortunately, the car handled great. If anything, we increased our lead after that pit stop.

When I took the white flag, Ray came on the radio with the sweetest words I'd ever heard: "One to go. And you're pulling away."

I would have answered him, but I couldn't speak for the

lump in my throat. I could barely see turn four of that final lap for the tears that had filled my eyes. When I crossed the finish line, I let it all go. Television cameras caught me sobbing, but I couldn't have cared less. As I said to the crowd when I finally made it the winner's circle, "This is the happiest day of my life. This is a memory and a feeling I'll never forget."

I wasn't the only one with tears on my cheeks that day. Mom and Brooke were watching with some of Mom's friends in one of the condos at the track. A friend listened to the finish over the scanner. When Mom saw her crying, she said, "What's the matter, Linda?"

"Jeff's crying," Mom's friend told her.

Mom joined her friend in a tearful moment.

Out on the track, I felt like a weight had been lifted off my back. The doubts, many of them self-imposed, were over. I finally knew we could win at this level. Needless to say, it was an emotional moment for all of us.

— — — —

If my first win was a sweet release after a year and a half of learning and growing in the sport, the second victory of my Winston Cup career was a historic homecoming, a thrill that eclipsed that first win in Charlotte.

During my rookie year, we had loaded up the hauler and taken a couple of cars north to Indiana for testing. What made the trip significant was where we were testing: the historic "Brickyard," the Indianapolis Motor Speedway, birthplace of modern racing, and home to the greatest spectacle in all of sports, the Indianapolis 500. The first time I went to the Indy

500, I remember leaning against the chain-link fence surrounding "Gasoline Alley" and watching my heroes go back and forth between garages. Rick Mears was the driver I admired the most. Getting his autograph that weekend made my heart race. I don't think I stopped smiling for a week.

Then we moved twenty miles away from the Speedway, and I spent my teenage years doing everything I could to be among the privileged few who trolled Gasoline Alley and drove across the two-foot-wide row of bricks at the start-finish line. In Indiana, the 500, as it's called, is more than a race: it's the state's identity. May, the month of the race, even takes on a special name. It's "the month of May," as if May were more important than the other eleven months. There was something mystic and magical about the Speedway, with its four distinct turns, short chutes, nine degrees of banking, and two and a half miles of history.

When I made the choice to race stockcars, I thought my dreams of racing at Indy were over. For eighty years, the only cars on that track were open-wheel Indy cars raced by guys like Johnny Rutherford and Rick Mears. When I ran my first test lap around the Brickyard in my DuPont 24 Chevrolet, I felt a chill run down my back.

A year later, in August of 1994, we were back for the Inaugural Brickyard 400. The Speedway sold 350,000 tickets, the largest crowd we'd ever had for a Winston Cup race. I was as excited and nervous as I had ever been before a race. As I told reporters in the media center, "To make history here in NASCAR is more than a dream come true."

The car that day was one we'd named *Booger,* and it was a great one. During practice, there wasn't anybody I couldn't run down. Once the race started, I caught an early break when Geoff and Brett Bodine bumped each other in turn two. The subsequent wreck almost took me out, but I was able to slide low and avoid getting tangled up with the brothers Bodine. I led more than half the laps that day—93 of 160 to be exact—but the only one that counted was the last one. With about twenty laps to go I looked in my mirror and saw Ernie Irvan pulling to my inside.

"Stay with him," Ray said.

This was Ray's way of reminding me that it was still early. We had a lot of racing left, and if I got too anxious and tried to pass Ernie too early, I might blow my chances at the end.

"Just stay with him," Ray said. The idea was to force Ernie to race me side by side on a high, outside line. With so little banking at Indy, taking a high line through the turns wreaks havoc on your tires. If I could make him run hard and high, we hoped to wear his tires down so that he would have to get out of the throttle. I stuck with him for sixteen laps of head-to-head racing. Then, with four laps to go, Ernie cut a tire, wobbled, and barely avoided the wall in turn two. It was unfortunate that Ernie blew a tire; it would have been great to race him all the way to the yard of bricks. As it was, I won the inaugural Brickyard 400 by four car lengths.

Afterward, I took one extra victory lap just to compose myself. I think most people understood why.

–   –   –   –   –

We finished eighth in the points race in 1994, a little more than nine hundred points behind Dale Earnhardt, who won his seventh Winston Cup title, joining Richard Petty as the only other seven-time champion in the sport. We had accomplished one of our goals; we had won two races and put up some good numbers throughout the year. But we had too many races we did not finish (DNFs) to be competitive for the championship. Ten times we had crashed, blown an engine, lost a transmission, or otherwise had mechanical failures that blew us out of the race. That was an unacceptably high number. If we'd just finished those races running, we would have had a shot at winning a lot of races. So consistency became the goal in 1995.

By our third year together, the team had gelled. Our philosophy of continuous, incremental improvement—making every week better than the one before, every outing, every pit stop, and every practice lap just a little bit stronger than the last one—had put us ahead of schedule. I figured if we stuck to our plan and remained focused on the task directly in front of us, we could realistically win a lot of races in 1995, and possibly contend for the championship.

I never said that out loud to anyone, especially not early in the year when I was less than six months removed from my twenty-third birthday. If I had mumbled to somebody that we might win the Winston Cup in 1995, I would have been laughed out of the garage. It's not like the team got together on January 1 and said, "This is the year." This team had really come together and we'd had a great off-season testing the new Monte Carlo. I figured if we took it one lap at a time, one race at a time, and focused all our energies and efforts on making the current lap better than the last one, and the next lap better than the current one, the rest of the pieces would fall into place. We would win our fair share of races, and if we did that, the championship would take care of itself.

– – – – –

There were plenty of hiccups along the way, like the first race of the year. We thought we finally had a chance to win the Daytona 500 in 1995. After testing great in January, we qualified fourth and kept getting better as the weekend progressed. It was one of those weekends where you could feel a win coming. Everything was clicking. The car was perfect, and I led for fifty laps.

Then I came in for a routine four-tire pit stop. As always, the right side of the car went up first and the crew quickly changed the right-side tires while the gasman filled the tank. The right side went down and I saw the Warriors scramble around to the left side. The car went up, and the tire changers went to work. What I didn't know was that the left-front tire guy was having trouble. He couldn't get the tire off, because one of the lugs was still in place. When he saw the problem, he leaned back to get the air gun to loosen the nut. The jackman saw him lean back, which was his cue to lower the car. He thought the tire had been changed and we were ready to go. When the jack lowered and all four tires were on the ground, I released the clutch and punched the throttle. That was my cue to get back out there.

Just as in Richmond the previous season, the tire came off before I made it out of the pits, and the car took some pretty good front-end damage. The crew hustled to get me back out on the track, but our chances of winning were over. We were all devastated that we'd had the car and lost it. I was frustrated and disappointed. Ray was livid. The calmest thing he said was "It's a shame. We had it, and we gave it away."

Fortunately, those kinds of mistakes were the exception instead of the norm for us in 1995. The wins came early and often. One week after our disaster in Daytona, we won the Good-wrench 500 at Rockingham. Two weeks later we won in Atlanta at the Purolator 500. A month into the season and we had already doubled our career Winston Cup victories. Two weeks later we made it three out of six with a win in Bristol, Tennessee, at the Food City 500.

This was one of those rolls, the kind of unexplainable streak where everybody on the team does everything right, and all the breaks seem to go our way. At the First Union 400 in North Wilkesboro, we won the pole and finished second. Then we finished third in Martinsville. A week later, we finished second on the Superspeedway at Talladega and, for the first time ever, took over the lead in the Winston Cup points race.

Actually we were tied for the lead with Dale Earnhardt, but the fact that we'd won more races than Dale at that point in the season gave us the edge. According to NASCAR rules, ties go to the guy with more wins. It was moot at that point in the year, since we still had twenty-two races to run, but that was when the first rumblings of a "rivalry" between Dale and me started making the rounds.

Of course I wanted to beat Dale, just like he wanted to beat me. We were competitors. I raced him hard, and he raced me hard. That's how we made our livings. To assume that I ramped my driving up a notch when Dale was on my rear, or that he elevated his driving when I was behind him, is an insult to the other drivers. It also shows a lack of understanding about our sport. Even if I had wanted to "take it to another level" when Dale was behind me, I couldn't, because I didn't have another level. I gave it everything I had in every race I ran from the moment the track went green until the checkered flag fell. To say that I took it to another level when Dale and I were battling in a race or for a championship is to assume that I was giving something less than my best the rest of the time. That's never been the case. I've always believed Dale raced the same way.

As I gained on Dale in the 1995 points battle, he brought out that nickname Wonderboy again. I just laughed about it, and we used it as a motivational tool in the garage. We were building a bit of a professional rivalry with the 3 car driven by Dale. He wanted to use that nickname as gamesmanship; we used it to fire up our team.

Dale had built a loyal following by positioning himself as "the Intimidator" and "the Man in Black." To his legions of fans he was the bad boy of racing. He was also trying to become the only man in history to win eight Winston Cup titles, breaking the record he shared with The King, Richard Petty. I guess a lot of fans took exception to a twenty-three-year-old nudging the Intimidator out of first place, but who knows? They might have taken exception to that I was from California while most of the other drivers were from the South. Plus, I didn't smoke, didn't chew tobacco, didn't go deer hunting, and would rather dive with a school of fish than sit in a boat and catch them. Dale's most rabid fans might have viewed all these traits as character flaws; at least that was the speculation at the time.

The more I won, the more fans I attracted, and the more people pulled against me. A lot of people loved that I was a young guy with a new team. Others might have thought I was destroying the fabric of the sport. This is when the first "Gordon Sucks" signs came out and the boo birds tuned up again when I was introduced.

At some point during this time (I have no idea exactly when), anti-Gordon fans started passing around the rumor that I was gay. I can only guess that it had something to do with my driving a rainbow-colored car. I also figure some folks took a joke Dale Earnhardt made during my rookie year out of context: I had been dating Brooke throughout the season, but because Winston employed her, we had to keep our relationship secret. After her stint as Miss Winston Cup ended, we came out at the banquet as a couple. Dale, being witty as ever, said, "Whew, I'm glad to see you've got a girlfriend. Some of us were beginning to wonder if you liked girls." Of course, Dale and a lot of other drivers had known about Brooke for months, but they hadn't said anything out of respect for our privacy. Once we showed up in public together, Dale felt comfortable making a joke about it. I can only guess that a few folks took him seriously, and the rumors about my sexual orientation spread like wildfire.

The controversy (such that it was) never bothered me, but I was a bit puzzled by it. I'd like to think if I were gay, I would be comfortable enough to say so and get on with my life. The fact is I'm not, and I never quite understood why so many people wanted to believe otherwise.

I was just being myself, doing what I'd always done, and giving it everything I had on race day. The thought of me being a polarizing figure was strange to me. I wasn't really prepared for it. I thought, "If I start winning, I'll attract fans." That happened, but I also became a target for a lot of people who needed a villain. One reporter wrote that the more I won, the more fans divided themselves into two camps: the "We Love Jeff Gordon" side and the "Anybody but Gordon" camp.

Fortunately, I gave people a reason to care. If I'd been running in the back of the pack every week, nobody would have bothered to make "We Hate Jeff" signs, and only a few people would have bought DuPont team jackets. As it was, our run from the last week in February of 1995 through the final race of the year on November 8, 1999, was one of the best in the history of racing, and a ride I would never have dreamed possible.

— — — —

At times in life the stars align, everything goes your way, every decision seems to be right, and every break falls in your favor. Some people call it being blessed, while others refer to it as destiny. Those are philosophical concepts I'm not smart enough to address, but I know what we achieved in that four-year stretch from 1995 through 1998 is pretty special. We worked our tails off to get where we did and put ourselves in a position to win a lot of races, and we were able to take advantage of the breaks when they came our way. I was also able to ride a wave of growing popularity in our sport and bring a lot of new fans to NASCAR. But at the end of the day, it was our team's performance that told the story.

In that four-year stretch, we won 40 races and had 98 top tens out of 127 races. We also led a total of 8,541 laps, which was more than our nearest two competitors combined. This would have been a pretty good record if only ten of us had been racing. With a full field of cars racing every week, it was one of those unbelievable streaks that was unheard of at the time.

We started our roll the second week of the 1995 season when we won the pole in Rockingham, led 329 of 492 laps, and won our third career race in commanding fashion. Two weeks later, we won again, this time starting on the side of the second row (third) and leading 250 of 328 laps in Atlanta. It had taken us two years to win two races, and then, suddenly, we broke out with two wins in four starts in 1995. Taking the checkered flag was fun; I wanted it to continue.

At the Food City 500 the first weekend in April, we made it three out of six, winning again after starting second and leading 205 of 500 laps. The season was less than two months old, and we already had one more win than we'd had in the previous two years. I just hoped we could keep doing things right for the rest of the year.

The only reason we weren't leading the points race at that stage was because we'd had two DNFs: one in Richmond, where we blew a fuel pump, and a second in Darlington, where we got caught up in a crash. After our win at Bristol, we trailed Dale Earnhardt by 156 points.

Three weeks later in Talladega, we took the points lead for the first time ever. After that, our confidence couldn't have been higher. Ray seemed to make all the right calls at the right times, and the team believed that if they could keep me in a good, fast car, I was going to have a chance at the end. I believed it, too. If I was somewhere close with a few laps to go, I thought we had a good shot at winning. Our confidence was high, and it positively affected everybody on our team.

We led at least one lap in twenty-nine of the thirty-one races we ran, and we led the most laps eleven times throughout the year. We won four more races, bringing our season win total to seven, and we won a total of eight poles for the year, something that hadn't been done in ten years, but I think I was most proud that we were competitive almost every week. From the first week of June through the first weekend in October, we were only out of the top ten once (a sixteenth at Pocono), and when the season ended, we had led 2,600 of 9,863 laps.

But we didn't have the best average finish of the year. That title went to Dale, who had a yearly average finish of 9.2 to our 9.5. For that reason, the points race was close to the very end. When the final points were tallied, we held off Dale by only thirty-four points, making this the eighth-closest points race in Winston Cup history.

A one-point victory would have been enough for me. We had our first championship. And Rick Hendrick had his first Winston Cup title.

At the banquet in New York I thanked Rick and everybody on our team who had made it possible for me to be at the head table that night. Then I said, "I would also like to recognize a man who never let up on his efforts to win his eighth championship. Dale Earnhardt is a true competitor and a great champion, and at this time I would like to offer a toast to 'The Man.' "

With that, I took the carton of milk that had been delivered to the stage in a champagne bucket—a joke thrown back at Dale Earnhardt, who had said earlier in the year, "Jeff is so young, I guess they'll have to serve milk instead of champagne at the banquet"—and raised a toast to Dale, a good friend, a great champion, and a worthy opponent.

– – – – –

My life was like a whirlwind after that first championship. The week of the banquet, I was on *The Late Show with David Letter-*

man and *Good Morning America,* where I tried to be funny, but probably came off a little stiff. This was the first time a lot of people outside the small, inside world of racing had ever seen me, and it was a whole new arena. Membership in my fan club grew by a factor of ten in the next few months, but I wasn't thinking about that. As I told David Letterman the Friday before our banquet, "This is too good to be true. There aren't words to describe how I feel. It's been a spectacular year, better than we ever thought it could be."

More than anything I was proud that we had validated Rick Hendrick's multicar philosophy. By having more than one team operating out of one facility, we proved that you could take the best from everybody and raise the standards for all. That proved true again in 1996 when my teammate Terry Labonte won the championship and I finished second. Now the idea that three teams out of one shop was unmanageable seemed silly. Rick had won two championships in a row and seemed poised to win many more. Our engine department was the best in the business. We were one of the first to employ full-time engineers, and one of the first to have a computer in our pit box. While other operations where using one or two fabricators, we had dozens, and our mechanics were the best in the business. Suddenly, ours was the operation everyone aspired to work for. The brightest wanted to join us. In my opinion, we were the best of the best in every category.

One of the consequences of our success, and one of many things I didn't expect at the time, was the amount of name and face recognition I would have, and the increased demands on my time. For the first time in my life, I had to hire a business manager who wasn't related to me. My mom and dad had done an outstanding job throughout my career, but the business had grown to a point where I needed someone to manage my business full-time. I hired a North Carolina banker and businessman named Bob Brannan to manage Jeff Gordon, Inc. and all its affiliated companies.

Being recognized has its price, but I've been lucky. Unless I'm in a racing town or at home, I can usually put on a cap and walk around without being universally recognized. There were some funny moments, though. My house on Lake Norman became a tourist stop for recreational boaters. One night I was at home trying to have a quiet dinner when I saw several white flashes out on the water. When I went out on my deck, I saw a stream of boats just beyond my pier. The owners were taking pictures and waving. "Oh, there he is," one of them yelled. I waved back, but turned the lights out and ate in the dark.

Another funny moment occurred when I was driving down I-77 in Charlotte one afternoon on my way home. A car that had been following me for a few miles pulled alongside me to pass. I didn't pay attention to the person behind the wheel, but I rarely do when I'm driving. I don't think many people look at the drivers of the other cars on the road. But the person who passed me obviously had. Once the car got by me, the driver hit the brakes. I passed the car, and it fell in behind me again. When I exited, the car exited. When I turned left over the overpass, it turned left with me. For a minute I was concerned. I didn't want whoever this was to follow me home, so I pulled into the parking lot of Taco Bell, stopped the car, rolled down my window, and waited. An excited man and women got out of the car and said, "Jeff, can we have your autograph?" I signed autographs for them, and they drove away happy. That one left me shaking my head. Not only would I never give more than a passing glance at the driver of another car on the interstate, the likelihood of me recognizing my best friend in that split second is pretty slim. I had to give this couple credit: they were observant, not to mention persistent.

For a while I lived in South Florida, so that when I was home, I could get away a little. I spent as much time as I could down there—I love Florida and think it's a great place to live— but I wasn't home as much as I would have liked. My home was still the motor coach. After a while I got used to the new demands of my lifestyle. The few hassles I've experienced are a small price to pay to be as successful as I've been in the profession that I love.

In 1997 and 1998 we went on a tear like nothing our sport had ever seen. We won twenty-three times in two years, a record for the modern era of the sport, and won championships in both seasons. I finally broke through and won my first Daytona 500 in 1997. But the 1998 season was particularly satisfying. Our team had been together five years at that point, and while we had made a few changes along the way, the key people had been working together for a long time. Everyone knew everyone else's moves, and most of us could anticipate the calls before Ray made them.

We took over the points lead in early May with a win in Charlotte and never let it go. When the dust finally settled, we'd won thirteen times. We'd also won four consecutive races in July and August and set several modern records. I became one of only seven drivers to win three or more Winston Cup titles.

A lot of people questioned the secret of our success. Was it the cars? Did Hendrick Motorsports have the magic formula for building the perfect racecar? Was it Ray Evernham? Did he know something the rest of the crew chiefs didn't? Was it me? Did I have something that the rest of the drivers didn't? I never answered those questions, because I thought all of them missed the point. It was none of those things and all of those things. It was the team that made us what we were. Without Rick Hendrick's commitment and obsession to being the best in the business, nobody would have been asking about our secret, because we wouldn't have been winning. Without team members like Brian Whitesell, who worked longer and harder than anybody else in racing, we wouldn't have been the envy of the Winston Cup garages.

My weight might have given us an advantage. With a full tank of gas, Winston Cup cars weigh thirty-four hundred pounds. When you add another two hundred for the driver, the car weighs thirty-six hundred pounds. I weigh a hundred and fifty pounds dripping wet in a race suit. At the time, that extra fifty pounds didn't sound like much, but in a five-hundred-mile race, every ounce made a difference. Now, NASCAR weighs both car and driver, so everybody starts with the same weight.

My size wasn't mentioned during our 1998 run, but that was the only theory that didn't get batted around. Some people said Hendrick Motorsports must have come up with some space-age technique for cutting down on drag. Others were calling Ray the best crew chief in the history of racing. But Jack Roush had a different theory.

Jack said to a television reporter with a camera, "The twenty-four car is running around there as a fourth-through-tenth-place car on four tires, and they put two tires on at the end and pick up seven—or eight-tenths of a second. That's really incredible. I don't know anyone else who can do that."

We were in New Hampshire, which was a track where you

could get away with a two-tire change because track position was so important. I felt that Jack should have known that, and I was sure he didn't mean for his comments to come across as rough as they did. But it was clear that he was accusing us of cheating.

I thought Jack's accusations stemmed from the fact that his number 6 car, driven by Mark Martin, was in second place at the time and losing ground every week. Jack had simply let his frustrations spill over.

At the AC Delco 400 in Rockingham, Ray confronted Jack and told him that he was mistaken. I don't know if Jack apologized at that time, but I feel certain that he now wishes he hadn't made those offhand remarks. The guy who really felt bad was Mark Martin, one of the true gentlemen of our sport. Mark felt terrible about what had happened and did the only thing he could: he and his crew chief, Jimmy Fennig, approached me and said, "Don't think this is coming from us." I didn't, and I told them so. Mark and Jimmy run a classy team, and I was glad they came by and talked to us.

Later that afternoon we clinched the championship with a down-to-the-wire win in Rockingham and, in so doing, became the first team in sixteen years to win thirteen races in a season.

At the postvictory press conference I could barely contain my glee. "Man, that was awesome," I said. "Ray Evernham and this team, they are awesome; they are what has made this year the year it has been. We were really blessed. What an awesome year; what an awesome championship!"

Through all my excitement I think I got it right that afternoon. We won our third Winston Cup championship that afternoon because no part of our team was any more or less important than any other.

Afterward, I remembered something I'd said at the banquet after our first championship. "How Ray and I met wasn't by luck," I'd told the crowd. "It was truly by fate, but we didn't know it until now."

Fate had brought this team together. Little did I know what the future held in store for us.

Five

Golden Rule

7 f you win, you're going to get scrutinized. No way around it. It doesn't matter if you're winning Winston Cup races, posting record earnings for the third consecutive quarter, or acing your fourth final exam in a row; people love to analyze winners. And in NASCAR, if you win one-third of the races in a year, people are going to look long and hard at how you did it.

I didn't have time to look back on what we'd done. My thoughts always centered on the next race, the next test, or the next qualifying or practice session. I said in an interview at the time, "I don't know that I'll really comprehend what it all means until later in life when I can sit back and look at everything we've accomplished." I'm older and hopefully wiser now, but I think I'm several years away from fully appreciating the magnitude of what we accomplished.

But the success was also a distraction. From the Monday after our last race in November until Speedweek in Daytona in February, I had to test new cars, follow through on my contractual commitments to sponsors, shoot commercials for DuPont and Pepsi as well as do promotional spots for NASCAR, close out the year-end books on my licensing and marketing businesses as well as my foundation and other business ventures, pay my taxes, buy Christmas presents, try to maintain a personal life, plus handle media requests that had tripled in twenty-four months. It was hectic and frustrating. I wish I'd had more time for reporters, fans, friends, and family members, but I also understood that the role of Winston Cup champion came with additional responsibilities.

I also expected the questions that followed. We had set a

pretty high bar, so when I was asked, "Is it impossible to top what you did last year?" I had a hard time answering because it was a question I'd been asking myself. The truth was, I didn't know if we could top what we'd done. The run we had been on was phenomenal, but those kinds of streaks are bound to end. Our goal was to win championships. If it took thirteen wins to accomplish that goal, that was our target. If one win got the job done, we were okay with that, too. We had to keep making our next race better than our last, taking it one lap, one race, at a time. If we continued to do the little things better than everybody else, we could keep the streak alive and make a run at our fourth championship.

But from the first weeks of 1999, I could tell things were different. What I didn't realize was how different they had become, or the impact those changes would have on all of us.

– – – –

The change started subtly, as these things often do. Rick Hendrick had sold us a concept of shared success, every team learning from the successes and failures of every other team. A rising tide lifts all ships, and we were definitely riding a tidal wave. The garages for all the Hendrick Motorsports teams were in the same complex with the engine and chassis departments, so everybody was within a two-minute walk of everybody else. In theory, Terry Labonte's engineer could walk over to our engineer and pick up any information he needed, and vice versa. If Terry's guys thought a softer shocks package was appropriate for Rockingham, everybody in the Hendrick Motorsports garage should have had access to that information and the logic behind it. We might disagree (which Rick never minded and often encouraged), but the information was there to see.

From my vantage point, the concept worked great. I always talked with my teammates, because I felt like I could learn something from other drivers. I knew I didn't know everything, and any tidbit I could pick up from a teammate—a feeling at a particular track, a throttle position, lines on a track—was useful. I was happy to share what I knew as well. That was what Rick's concept was all about, and by 1999 we'd proven that multiple-car teams worked.

Ray agreed with it, too. He'd seen the benefits of sharing information and resources, and he knew that we were much better off in this multiple-team arrangement than we would have been in a one-car operation. But he also wanted the best for our team, and there were some decisions that were made that Ray, had he been in charge, might have done differently. Sharing was fine, as long as our team always had the best stuff.

Ray didn't wake up one morning after our third championship and say, "I want more control, and I want our team to be the A team at Hendrick." Ray was never rude or unprofessional, and he certainly wasn't insubordinate. He continued to do everything in his power to win races for Hendrick Motorsports, and he ran the shop with the same intensity that had brought the two of us together. What he didn't do was embrace every decision in the free-flowing information model.

Don't get me wrong; it wasn't a big conflict. Rick continued to be thrilled with our performance. Rick and Ray were friends then and remain friends to this day. Any insinuation otherwise is not only just plain wrong, it also misses the point. The problem was, Ray had grown to a point in his life and career where he wasn't satisfied being one of Rick's crew chiefs. Ray wanted to be an owner.

— — — — —

Late in 1998 Ray and I started talking about forming our own Busch racing team. I don't remember who broached the subject first, but we both thought it was a great idea. PepsiCo, one of my longtime sponsors, wanted more on-car exposure and brand connection with me, and a Busch car seemed like the perfect answer. I could race a limited Busch schedule (we settled on six races) with Pepsi as the primary sponsor. The rest of the season we thought we could use the car as a sort of "farm league" for promising young drivers who might work their way into the Hendrick Motorsports operation. We started with Ricky Hendrick, Rick's son, as the driver.

It didn't take long to work out the details. I would drive in six Busch races with Pepsi as the sponsor, and Ricky would drive the remainder of the season with GMAC sponsoring the car. We would keep the number 24, but Ray, my wife, Brooke, and I would own the car. We formed Gordon-Evernham Motorsports, GEM, and got under way with the blessing and help of Rick Hendrick.

I thought the whole idea was neat because I loved Busch racing, and six more days of racing could do nothing but help me. Plus, I was helping out one of my best sponsors. If there was a downside, I couldn't see it.

What I didn't notice was Ray's growing restlessness. We had been together six years, five of them working for Rick Hendrick, and Ray was looking for the next mountain to climb. That was just part of his personality. Ray had always been this way. He always wanted to improve. Just like me, he had been thrilled when we won our first championship, but Ray didn't particularly like the way we finished that season with a weak October. It wasn't my preference, either, but, heck, we still had the trophy. Ray analyzed that year just as he analyzed our performances each week and said, "Okay, how can we do it better next time?"

The way we won in 1998 was more like it. Ray was the kind of competitor who believed that when you had an opponent down, you kept him down until you finished him off. He also thrived on being challenged. The more we achieved, the more he wanted to go to the next level. After thirteen wins in 1998, that bar was pretty high. And Ray started looking for another challenge.

Everybody in racing knew that Dodge was getting back into NASCAR. They had won a lot of championships, but hadn't been a factor in Winston Cup in more than decade. Now, they wanted back into the sport in a big way. I'm not sure when the folks at DaimlerChrysler approached Ray, but I understood why they did. If they wanted to make a bold statement, putting an ownership deal together with Ray Evernham was the perfect way to do it.

I made it clear to Ray from the beginning that I wasn't interested in starting a new team with Dodge or anyone else at the time. In the past I had looked at a couple of ways of getting into Formula One and decided that I was better off staying in Winston Cup. With that decision behind me, there was no question that I wanted to stay with Rick Hendrick. I hoped Ray felt the same way.

Once February rolled around, I didn't give it much thought. The only thing on my mind was making another run at the Daytona 500. I'd won NASCAR's biggest event in 1997, and I'd won the Pepsi 400 at Daytona in October of 1998, so I felt good about our chances. What I didn't expect was to be involved in one of the classic duels in Winston Cup history.

− − − − −

We won the pole for the Daytona 500 and were focused on putting the best car out on the track for the biggest race of the season. When the race started, I knew we had a good car, but I thought we'd blown our chances early when we received a fifteen-second penalty from NASCAR for having too many guys over the wall at once. The limit is seven—four tire changers, one jackman, a gasman, and a catch-can man who stands behind the car holding a container to catch any gas overflow that might ignite or cause the pit box to become slick if it spills. Somehow, we had eight guys over the wall at once—a bone-headed mistake that can only be compared to having six men on a basketball court or thirteen men on a football field at once.

I sat in the cockpit fuming. Fifteen seconds is an eternity in Winston Cup racing. When I got back out there, we were on the tail end of the lead lap.

When I got back out after the penalty, I was doing my best to block the leaders so I wouldn't get lapped. Daytona is one of the two superspeedways on the Winston Cup circuit (the other is Talladega Superspeedway in Alabama). The old definition of a superspeedway was any track over a mile in length, but that definition changed as more high-banked tracks of a mile or more were built. Talladega and Daytona are the longest tracks with the highest degrees of banking, which means they would be the fastest tracks we race on, except for one thing: the restrictor plate. In 1988, NASCAR officials decided that 210 miles per hour was too fast, even for a sport built on speed, so they required metal plates be added to the carburetors when we raced at Daytona and Talladega. Those plates cut the horsepower from 750 to just over 450. That slows everybody down, but it also forces the cars to run closer together. Without enough acceleration to push the car into the lead, running close together and drafting is one of the only ways to improve track position. Once you get a lap down in a restrictor-plate race, your day is pretty much over. After our penalty, I knew I had to keep the leaders behind me if I was going to have any chance.

It was nip and tuck for a few laps, but I was able to stay on the lead lap until we got another caution. That was a huge break. We had a good car. Now that we weren't fighting to hold our lead-lap position, I thought we could make some progress.

I was able to find drafting partners throughout the day and avoid the inevitable pileups that restrictor-plate racing creates. Since paring back the horsepower cuts down on the average speed and bunches up the cars, it also makes it hard to get out of the way when there's a wreck. Almost every restrictor-plate race has at least one big crash with a lot of cars involved, a fact of life when you run a lot of laps as close together as we do. We all know the Big One is coming. You just do what you can to avoid being in it.

I only led 6 of the first 189 laps, but with only 11 laps to go I liked our chances. We had worked us back into the top three thanks to some good breaks and great teamwork.

In the tri-oval of lap 190, I had to make a choice. Rusty Wallace was leading and Mike Skinner was making a move to the outside. We had lap traffic just ahead, so if I let Rusty take the low line and race Mike through turn two, I would be trapped in third place without much hope of making another run. If I took the low line, I would have to pass Rusty quickly to avoid Ricky Rudd, who was coming off of pit road on the apron.

With only ten laps to go, the choice was pretty easy. This was before the "yellow line" rule at Daytona where drivers are penalized for driving below the yellow line. I dove low and slid beneath Rusty at the entry of turn one, while Mike took the high line. We were three wide through the middle of the turn, and Ricky's car was coming up on us quick.

This one was going to be tight. I didn't want to make such a tight move, especially since I knew Mike was heading high, but I had too much momentum. It was now or never. There's a lot of apron at the bottom of the track at Daytona and I used every inch of it.

I bet I didn't miss Ricky by more than a couple of inches.

Mike was still high, Rusty was in the middle, and I had the low line. We were three-wide for almost a full lap.

When I checked my mirror I saw Dale Earnhardt right on my tail. He was so close I couldn't see the Goodwrench logo on the hood of his car, but I didn't care. Dale took just enough air off my spoiler to allow me to make a run.

Two years before, Terry Labonte and I had been in a similar situation at the same time in the race. Terry and I were teammates. When we finally caught the leader, Bill Elliott, on lap 190, we went low and used our aerodynamic momentum to push by him. Then Terry and I raced to the finish, and I won my first Daytona 500. The big difference in that move and the one I was making now was that Bill Elliott knew Terry and I had built up enough momentum to get by him so he went high and let us pass. When Dale and I went low, Rusty had gone low and tried to block us.

By the entry of turn two, Rusty had taken a slightly higher line. That was all the room we needed. I shot past with Earnhardt right behind me.

Afterward Rusty said, "I just couldn't block him off enough. I'm just brokenhearted that this happened. I thought about just holding him down on the apron and driving him right into the back of Rudd's car. I thought Gordon would maybe get out of the throttle a little bit, but he wouldn't. To do it over again, I probably would have held him down there and waited for the outcome."

Rusty also thought my move was a little too aggressive for the situation. I was aggressive, but those are the moves you have to make to win in that situation. It wouldn't have been quite so aggressive if Rusty had given me a little more room. As it was, I slipped below Rusty and Mike, and a few inches above Ricky. The move had the crowd on their feet.

Once Dale and I got clear of Rusty, we stopped being drafting partners and became head-to-head competitors for the win. Adding to the drama was the fact that Dale had won his first Daytona 500 in 1998, and I'd won my first in 1997. We were the past two defending champions, and we had ten Winston Cup championships between us. You couldn't have scripted it better.

Dale tried to work beneath me at the entry of every turn, but my car was good enough in the center of the turns that I was able to block him. As we drove out of the turns, I was able to put some distance between us on the straightaways. But Dale would catch me at the beginning of every turn and make his move. I was just able to hold him off.

We were still battling when we took the white flag. With one lap to go, I didn't know what to expect. If I could hold him off through four more turns, I'd have it. I wasn't sure of the outcome until we exited turn four. When he couldn't get by me on that last effort (although we were rubbing), I knew I had my second Daytona 500 win in three years.

That was one of the most satisfying wins of my career. To make the move we made with ten laps to go, then race Dale Earnhardt to the finish, was what makes winning so great. This was one for the history books. It felt great to come out on top.

Not long after that race, several NASCAR people who own boats went down to the Bahamas for a little fun and relaxation. I don't normally hang out with other drivers when I'm away from the track, not because we're not friends, but because when I'm away from the track, I like to get away. That has changed a little recently, as Jimmie Johnson and I have become close buddies. We both have friends in New York, and we hang out a lot together in the city, but for the first eight years of my Winston Cup career, I had my track friends and my away-from-the-track friends, and the two rarely crossed paths. So, it was great to get away with some of the drivers for a little diving and non-race-related fun.

While we were there, I went diving with Rusty Wallace and Michael Waltrip. We went down about thirty feet and I took out my underwater camera to shoot some of the beautiful fish, coral, and rock formations in the crystal-clear water. As I was shooting, our guide tapped me on the shoulder and motioned for me to give him the camera. When I did, he handed me a Pepsi can and gave Rusty a Miller beer can, and the two of us had our photo taken sitting on the ocean floor holding up products of our respective sponsors. I still have that photo, and I show it to people often as an illustration of how drivers can be fierce competitors on the track and good friends when we park the cars in the garage.

I'm not sure Rusty would have considered me a buddy after my win at Daytona. And I don't think I would have been so ecstatic after that win if I had known the trying times that were coming my way. Daytona was a great win. Too bad it was the highlight of our season.

— — — — —

We had a poor showing at Rockingham, where we blew an engine and finished thirty-ninth, but we came back and finished third in Las Vegas and won our second race of the year in Atlanta at the Cracker Barrel 500. A week later we won the pole and finished third at Darlington. It looked like we were on pace for another great year. We trailed Jeff Burton in the Cup race by a measly seven points, and through five races we had two wins and four top fives, the kind of start we'd had when we won those championships. It looked as though we had picked up right where we'd left off.

We also had a good start in our Busch car. I qualified second in Las Vegas and finished the race in fourth place. Four weeks later in Texas, I started fourth, but the car had some handling problems and we finished thirteenth.

In the Busch series, I started noticing the biggest change in

Ray. My first hint at the future came in Charlotte during testing. Ray was standing on the transporter with his hands on his hips surveying the area, and you could see the joy in his face. This was where he wanted to be. He was a team owner, and he liked it. When he came back to the garage that afternoon, he was like a proud father. Although I didn't want to admit it, I knew where Ray and I were headed after that test.

We did a good job keeping our Busch and Cup operations separate, but we started having some problems in our Winston Cup car the sixth week of the season in Texas. After qualifying eighth and having some great hot laps during happy hour (the final hour of practice before an event, usually held in the late afternoon when the track is cooling down and the speeds are going up), we cut a tire coming out of turn four only sixty-nine laps into the race. Because of where I was at the time, the car slid up the high banking and slammed into the turn-four wall. I hit hard and bruised my ribs pretty badly. Not only did we finish forty-third, our worst finish ever, I had sustained my first injury in a Winston Cup crash.

Six more times that season we either crashed or had mechanical problems that knocked us out of contention. On the days we did run well, Dale Jarrett, who was having a phenomenal season, ran as well or better and we were unable to gain any ground. We didn't do much better in the Busch car. In Charlotte, we had a rear-end problem that knocked us down to thirty-third place, and when Ricky Hendrick made his debut in the car in July in Myrtle Beach, he finished three laps down in twentieth place.

Throughout this time, Dodge was talking to Ray, and he was examining his options while I was renegotiating my contract to remain with Rick Hendrick. I have to admit that being a team owner had its advantages. I'd been driving competitively since I was five years old. At twenty-eight it was a little early to start thinking about retirement, but I certainly didn't see myself driving when I was forty-five. It was never too early to start asking myself, What's next? Where did I want to be in ten years?

There's a golden rule in business. In racing, as with any business, he who has the gold makes the decisions. By 1999, I had more money than I had ever dreamed existed, but I was still a contracted employee of Hendrick Motorsports. Rick was the owner. He made the decisions. I'd seen Richard Petty, the godfather of our sport, make a successful transition from driver to team owner, and Dale Earnhardt, although still racing for Richard Childress, had built Dale Earnhardt Incorporated (DEI) into one of the most impressive operations in racing. Dale's garage was fondly referred to as the Garage Mahal. These guys had made the transition from driver to driver/owner. Could I do the same thing? And is that what I truly wanted?

Those were the questions I asked myself as I was negotiating my future with Rick. I'd decided not to move to Europe and try getting into Formula One, and I certainly didn't want to go out on my own and start a new race team from scratch. I wanted to be a racecar driver, but I also wanted a plan for my future that would extend beyond being *just* the driver.

This went on for months. In the meantime, I had a Winston Cup car to drive for Rick Hendrick and a Busch car that needed my attention. Despite more DNFs than we'd had since my sophomore year in Winston Cup, we won a series-leading seven poles and four more races before the second week in August. And in the Busch car I made my fourth start in Michigan in August and finished second after a great one-on-one duel with Dale Earnhardt Jr. But the questions continued to swirl in my head.

I think Rick was taken aback that Ray was talking to Dodge, which was a little surprising. Little happens on the Winston Cup circuit without word getting around. When Rick found out, he could have gotten angry, but he didn't. He simply let the process run its course. If Ray wanted to stay, Rick would talk to him about his staying. If he wanted to leave to form his own team, Rick would talk to him about that as well.

I certainly looked at other options during that time, and I know it concerned Rick that both Ray and I were even considering a move. Rick had seen plenty of drivers leave over the years. Darrell Waltrip won three championships while driving for Junior Johnson, but didn't win any while he was driving for Rick. Benny Parsons had left. But perhaps the greatest heartbreak Rick had experienced was the sad story of Tim Richmond. From everything I've read and heard about him, Tim came to Winston Cup from Indy racing where he was considered a prodigy. In 1980, he had finished ninth in the Indy 500 and won the Rookie of the Year title. After crossing the yard of bricks at Indy that year, Tim's car ran out of gas on the backstretch, so he pulled over and flagged down the winner, Johnny Rutherford. A photo still hangs in the Indianapolis Motor Speedway museum of Tim riding to Victory Lane on the wing of Johnny Rutherford's car. That was Tim: happy, and hard not to like.

Rick called him "the greatest talent I've ever seen." And Tim had the wins to back it up. He made the transition from Indy to Winston Cup without missing a beat. Rick said he hoped to build the franchise around Tim. Then, suddenly, something happened. According to Rick, Tim's behavior became erratic. He would fall asleep in the transporter moments before he was supposed to qualify the car. He would disappear for days without anybody knowing where he was. He would snap at reporters and give bizarre ramblings on those occasions when he did give interviews. According to Rick, at one point Tim got in his mother's sedan and chased a *USA Today* reporter through his neighborhood because the guy was camped outside his house. Then, out of the blue, he resigned from Hendrick Motorsports and, for all practical purposes, dropped out of sight. Nobody saw him or heard from him for months. When the rest of the folks in the garage finally did hear from him, it was too late. Tim died of AIDS. He had been suffering from the effects of the disease and the drugs he took to control it, and he was either too proud or too afraid to tell anyone.

On the day Tim died, Rick was at the track entertaining Tom Cruise, who would play a character loosely based on Tim for the movie *Days of Thunder*. Tom's movie had a happy ending. Tim's life did not. And Rick never fully got over the loss.

Now Rick Hendrick was struggling with his own problems. He'd had leukemia for over a year, and the effects had drained him. He had an office in his house so he could work between naps. He would come to the track when he could, but rarely did he make it to the garage or the pits. When we won the Daytona 500, I spoke to Rick on the phone, and he was pretty excited. I told him that we missed him in Victory Lane. He said, "Not as much as I missed being there." That was a pretty emotional moment for us.

Rick, Ray, and I had always had more than an owner/crew-chief/driver relationship. Ray's son also battled leukemia, so

Ray and Rick would talk for hours about the disease and its treatments. The bond there transcended racing. I couldn't imagine any of us breaking that bond.

– – – – –

On Friday night, September 10, 1999, Ray came to my hotel room in Richmond, Virginia, with a briefcase and a smile. In the briefcase was a contract. He laid out Dodge's offer. "I'm going to do this deal," he said. "You can still come with me."

At the time, I didn't know that Ray had already approached my dad about being a partner in his new race team. John and my mom lived in London, where John worked for Action Performance, a souvenir and merchandizing company that licenses about 90 percent of the NASCAR and Winston Cup products sold around the world. According to John, Ray told him that he intended to sign a contract with Dodge. Ray asked John to join him. According to John's account, his answer was "Ray, I don't know of any close friendships that survive business partnerships. I'd rather stay your friend than become your partner."

In a way, that summed up how I felt, too. Ray and I had been friends, partners, team members, and champions. We had been to the top of the mountain together. Now it was time to go our separate ways. I was happy for Ray, and he said he was happy for me. I could tell he was excited about moving on. It was a great opportunity for him, just as staying with Rick Hendrick was a great opportunity for me. Ray and I shook hands and wished each other luck. It was one of the oddest feelings I've ever had.

We started sixth in Richmond that Saturday and finished fortieth after breaking a transmission with ninety laps to go.

The next morning I drove straight to Rick Hendrick's house. Rick was in bed when I got there, but he got up and met me at the door.

"What's wrong?" he said. Just like Rick: he was the one with leukemia, but he wanted to know what was wrong with me.

I took a deep breath and said the words I never thought I would have to say: "We've got to find a new crew chief. I'm staying. But Ray's leaving."

Six

Behind
the Curve

My mind was rushing at a thousand thoughts a minute. Rick and I talked about our next steps, and what we could expect from our team. We also talked about how we would go about searching for a new crew chief without alerting the rest of the racing world that we were in turmoil. At that time, we figured Ray would stay through the end of the year, but we needed his replacement in-house as soon as possible.

Rick had some iced tea in his refrigerator, and I remember drinking two or three glasses as we talked. To tell you the truth, this chat was as much about me talking through our new reality as it was about giving Rick the news about Ray Evernham. Ray had been the only crew chief I'd ever had in Winston Cup. He was a confidant, a partner, and someone I looked to as a younger version of my dad. Ray's decision to leave was as big a personal blow to me as it was a professional hit for our team. This talk with Rick was as much about my own peace of mind as it was about strategies for our future.

When Ray got back to Charlotte, he was upset that I had told Rick about his decision to leave. "You should have given me a chance to tell him myself," Ray said. "That's my job."

Ray was right. I should have let him sit down with Rick and explain the decision in his own words. It was a mistake on my part, but one born of good intentions. I knew word would filter back to Rick sooner rather than later. We needed to get in front of the situation and talk through things.

For months, Rick and I had talked at length about my future with Hendrick Motorsports and my desire to become more than just the driver of the 24 car, and we had worked out a plan for me to assume an equity stake in my team. I would be a driver/ owner after all. I would be an equity partner with Rick Hendrick in the operation I'd always considered the best in the business. Rick had been prepared to offer a similar arrangement to Ray, but Ray wanted his own team. Now he would have it. And I would be listening to someone new on the headset for the first time in nine years.

The mood was awkward for a while when Ray returned. He was rightfully upset, and disappointed. "Look," I told him. "I'm sorry I told Rick about this before you had a chance to, but you're leaving and I needed to talk to him about getting a new crew chief." We also needed to know who was going to leave and who planned to stay. I knew some of the guys were Ray's guys and would go with him, but others were loyal to Rick Hendrick and the 24 team and would stay. I wasn't going to be hurt if guys left. I understood it. We just needed to know who was leaving and who was staying so we could plan our future.

Plus, we still had Cup races to run and a Busch team to manage. I was 459 points behind Dale Jarrett with nine races to go. I wasn't mathematically out of the running, but for all practical purposes we had stopped focusing on the championship. I just didn't want the off-track distractions to spill over into the garage. I wanted the focus to return to the racetrack. In hindsight, I should probably have realized that wasn't going to happen.

Keeping a secret on the Winston Cup circuit is all but impossible. I expected rumors to trickle through the garages. The media got wind of our situation a couple of weeks after Ray and I had our meeting in Richmond, and the feeding frenzy was spectacular. I remember saying to one of the guys in my office,

"Is there nothing going on in our little world more interesting than this?"

Unfortunately, most of the reports were wrong. One news outlet reported that Ray and I had been feuding, and I had pressured Rick to fire him. Another took the opposite take: Ray had gotten fed up with my whining and quit in a huff. Internet sites speculated that Ray was tired of me getting all the credit for our success, while others said I had demanded a new crew chief because Ray was getting too much of the glory.

What wasn't funny was the distraction that ensued. We qualified nineteenth at New Hampshire, but it was evident that our nondenial denials weren't cutting it with the racing press. Ray's departure was the worst-kept secret in NASCAR, and all the tiptoeing we tried to do that week wore us down. We had a good car, and I finished fifth, cutting forty points off Dale Jarrett's lead, but that finish seemed lost in all the speculation about our future.

That was when Rick knew he had to act. We had all hoped that Ray could finish out the year with us, but the speculation and distractions were too great. Plus, Ray needed to focus his attention on his new team. He had a garage to outfit, a team to assemble, a driver to hire, sponsorships to sell, and a fleet of cars to build. It didn't make sense for him to stay around, especially with the distractions he would face from the outside, and the disruption it might cause in our shop.

Ray's contract with Hendrick Motorsports ran through 2006. If Rick had been so inclined, he could have held Ray to the term of his contract and tied Dodge up in court through most of the 2000 season. But that wasn't Rick's style. Once he knew of Ray's intentions, the two of them sat down in Rick's office and agreed to part friends. Dover, the last weekend in September, would be Ray's last race with the DuPont 24 Chevrolet. After that, he would take more of an advisory role. If I wasn't going to have him making the calls the rest of the year, I needed to get used to his replacement.

– – – – –

Brian Whitesell had been with us from the beginning. A Virginian and mechanical engineer whose senior design project at Virginia Tech had been to build, drive, and serve as crew chief on a SAE Mini Baja racecar, Brian had got into Winston Cup racing as a volunteer on Alan Kulwicki's team while he paid the bills as a test engineer for Mack Trucks. He was the spotter on Alan's 1992 championship team when he caught Ray's eye. Ray somehow convinced Brian, one of the sharpest engineers going, to come to Hendrick Motorsports as the truck driver. He also served as the timer and chassis technician, but his principal job was to get the transporter to the track every week. This was a guy who loved the sport and would do whatever it took to be part of a winning team.

When Rick became the first owner to have full-time engineers for each team, Brian was the perfect fit. He served as our team engineer through all three of our championship runs and was named Western Auto's Mechanic of the Year in 1997. Brian's wife, Mary, volunteered to cook our meals when we were on the road so that she could be part of the team and travel with Brian. After we all agreed that Ray would leave, Brian was the perfect choice to be my crew chief for the remainder of the season.

Ray gave Brian the news, which he took with gracious professionalism. Being a crew chief was not Brian's ultimate ambition. He had never jockeyed for the job and had been offered the job of crew chief for another team and turned it down. Brian was as loyal as anyone in our operation. At Dover, we asked him to become fill-in crew chief even though Ray was still on-site. Brian stepped in and made the calls without missing a beat.

We qualified with a time of 22.692 (158.646 miles per hour), which was seventh quickest. When the green flag fell on race day, we moved up quickly, passing Rusty Wallace on lap ten to move into second. Two laps later, I got around Tony Stewart and took the lead. But the car got tighter as the day wore on, and I gave the lead back to Tony and Mark Martin, who swapped the top spot for thirty laps. When Dave Marcis hit the inside wall, everybody pitted for the first time.

Brian called for some pretty major adjustments because we had been fighting handling problems. When I went back out, the car was tighter than it was before. I had to get out the throttle earlier in each turn to keep the front end from sliding up the track and into the wall. In the next thirty laps we went from fourth to twenty-third and were backing up fast. I told Brian the car needed something. We agreed to come into the pits, even though nobody else was pitting, to try to loosen the car. A fifteen-second pit stop dropped me down to thirty-eighth place. After another green-flag stop (this one scheduled for tires and gas), I fell four laps down.

I was frustrated, and I let a little desperation slip into my voice. At this point, Brian could easily have given up. He'd been thrown into a situation he didn't expect, and certainly one he hadn't gone looking for. But he hung in there and worked the problem, never losing his cool and always keeping the team focused on making things better.

Every adjustment we made late in the day seemed to make the car better. With ninety laps to go we broke back into the top twenty-five. When everyone else came in for the final round of green-flag pit stops on lap 339, Brian decided that we should stay out on the track. It was a risky call, but one that worked out for us. Fifteen laps later, Ricky Craven (who is one of my best friends in the garage) spun out, bringing out a caution flag and allowing us to pit without losing position. When we got out of the pits, we were in nineteenth place. On the final ten laps I was able to pick up two more spots to finish seventeenth.

It wasn't great. It wasn't even good by our standards, but under the circumstances, with Ray in uniform on the sidelines and the rumors swirling like a thundercloud over us, Brian and the team put out a gutsy performance. They took a car that was ill-handling, struggled with it all day, then fought back, never giving up until the last lap of the race.

I felt good about the team spirit we'd shown that day. But I couldn't help questioning our future.

— – — – —

The following Tuesday, Rick and Ray made it official, issuing a joint statement and taking questions from the media. Rick said, "Sometimes it's best to help someone with their ambitions, even if it may not be what you would hope for at the time. Ray let us know he had reached a point where he didn't want to be a crew chief anymore. In response to that, we were planning to move him up in the organization, but he decided he wanted to pursue having a team of his own."

Ray was gracious in his remarks: "This was my idea. And I am thankful that Rick is willing to work with me in a goal I have of running my own operation. I'm also thankful that he enabled me to work with Jeff Gordon, who is an incredible winner and maybe the best talent this sport has ever seen, as well as the 24 car crew. Jeff and that crew will be winning races for a long time to come. I was given a great opportunity to move up here at Hendrick. I can't imagine a greater person or a finer organization than Rick Hendrick and Hendrick Motorsports, and I know I would have had the best environment possible here. There is no one else I would consider working for."

Then Rick turned to the future: "We have a lot of confidence in Brian Whitesell. And especially important is the fact that Jeff Gordon does as well. We are confident in his abilities because he has already proven himself to us." Brian would play a vital role on our team for years to come, but none bigger than the job he would do as interim crew chief.

I jumped in at that point and gave a public vote of confidence for Brian: "I have tremendous confidence in Brian. I'm looking forward to many more wins and championships with him and our team. We've got a great organization. I'm looking forward to the future."

Ray also agreed to sell me his share of our Busch team, so we could dissolve GEM. We continued to race the Pepsi car for the rest of the year (I won the final Busch race I ran), but with that car being a Chevrolet and Ray's new deal being with Dodge, there were some difficulties. As with the rest of our history, Gordon-Evernham Motorsports split amicably, and everyone went his separate way.

— — — — —

What I didn't expect and couldn't have predicted in a million years was the kind of start we had with Brian at the helm. Less than a week after Ray made his final trip down Papa Joe Hendrick Drive, leaving our compound forever, Brian made one of the gutsiest calls I'd ever seen from a rookie crew chief. On the short track of Martinsville, where tires wear quickly, slipping and sliding goes on most of the day. With twenty-eight laps to go, the leaders in the NAPA AutoCare 500 came in for a scheduled four-tire pit stop. But just as he had done at Dover, Brian called for me to stay out on the track. It was a huge gamble once again. Without fresh tires, I might not have had enough grip to hold my position. Brian thought the tires were good enough, and staying out would give us the lead.

He thought we could hold it, and he was right. We stunned the racing world by winning our first week out with a new crew chief. "It just goes to show you what this team is made of," I said at the time. "With any change comes new challenges, and this team stepped up to the plate and got the job done. The team really rallied around Brian and me, and our communication has been great."

One week later we proved that the win wasn't a fluke. At the fall race in Charlotte, and only two days after announcing to the racing world that I had signed a lifetime contract with Hendrick Motorsports to be an equity partner and drive the 24 car for the rest of my career, we qualified twenty-second, but had a good car from the outset. Brian and the crew worked great all day. Not only do I believe they were on a high from the win in Martinsville, I think the newness of having Brian in charge made them a little quicker and little more alert than they might otherwise have been.

The car got better as the day wore on, and we made steady progress. I worked up through the field, picking up eight spots in the first ten laps, and getting progressively better. We were in the top ten by the hundred-lap mark, and we stayed there the rest of the race. Brian did a great job moving the car closer and closer to perfect as the race went on. When we pitted on lap 157, he adjusted the air pressure in all four tires. I got back on the track and felt an immediate difference. The car was as good as it had been all day, and at just the right time.

Jeff Burton spun out on lap 198, bringing out a caution. I made my move on the restart, pulling underneath Bobby Labonte to take the lead for the first time. I lost the lead one more time, but the crew got me in and out of the pits faster than any other car during our final pit stop. We closed up on some lap traffic, and I passed Bobby again with only seven laps to go. After leading only seven laps all day, I was leading with seven to go.

It was a tight finish. Bobby worked as hard as he could to get the lead back, but our car was too strong on the final laps, and just like that we won our second race in a row with Brian as crew chief. It was our seventh win of the year and moved us into fourth place in the points race.

Unfortunately, that was as close to Dale Jarrett as we would get. In the final five races of the year, our best finish was tenth (which we did twice, in Phoenix at the DuraLube 500 and a week later at Homestead in the Pennzoil 400). When we blew an engine at the season-ending race in Atlanta for our seventh DNF of the year, we were 642 points behind Dale and in sixth place.

Given the turmoil we'd had throughout the year, I guess that wasn't bad, but it certainly wasn't the kind of finish I liked. It had been five years since I'd finished a season worse than second. Sixth was respectable, but nowhere close to our capabilities.

– – – – –

Like in any small, highly specialized business, a lot of personnel swapping occurs in Winston Cup racing. Mechanics or over-the-wall crew members who have an opportunity to make the jump to a winning team do so quite regularly. At times it gets to be like musical chairs. One week a guy is working for team A, and the next week you see him suited up at the track for team B. Of course, it's not like you can run an ad on Monster.com for a catch can man or a racecar fabricator. These are specialized fields, and the universe of people who can do these jobs at the highest level is pretty small. We had been lucky. In five years of Winston Cup racing, Ray had been able to attract the best in the business, and we'd had an extremely low turnover rate. When you became a Rainbow Warrior, you knew you were in it for the long haul.

That's why it came as such a shock when our entire over-the-wall crew quit at the end of the 1999 season. I would have understood if we'd been mired in a two-year losing streak. Heck, I would have shaken their hands and said, "Good luck," if that had been the case. But we were the winningest active team in Winston Cup racing, second only to David Pearson on the all-time winning-percentage list, and seventh overall in career victories. Jumping off a sinking ship was one thing; but leaving the best operation in Winston Cup racing was a decision I didn't understand.

I might also have understood if all the crew had left with

Ray. He had hired most of them, and he'd been the only boss many of them had ever known. If he'd lured them away, I wouldn't have been happy, but I would have understood the logic behind their decision. Ray had taken some of our guys; he and they were up-front about their intentions, but he wouldn't have taken our entire pit crew.

That the pit crew left to join Robert Yates Racing and, more specifically, Dale Jarrett's car hurt me. Sure, Dale had just won the championship with a career year, but Rick Hendrick had won the previous four in a row. The only reasoning I could come up with for this decision was that this incarnation of our pit crew felt like our success was because of Ray Evernham. Once Ray left, they figured our future wasn't as promising.

I was pissed off. I never want anybody in our organization to think one person is responsible for our success or failure. We win and lose not just *as* a team, but because we *are* a team. If one person overshadows the team, we all suffer.

When I learned about the crew's decision, I talked to our key guys. "Ray had a great opportunity," I told them. "And we've had a great run. How we stick together now and work through this adversity is going to determine our future." It wasn't exactly the Gettysburg Address, but I got the message across.

Every racing reporter in the country picked up the story of my crew quitting, and by the time the story played out, you would have thought we were going to close the shop and retire. There was nothing I could say to sway their views. We would just have to prove them wrong on the track.

But we still had to find a crew chief. Brian Whitesell had done a fantastic job in an almost impossible situation at the end of the 1999 season. He was a spectacular engineer and team manager, but we needed someone who was as much an artist as a strategist, someone who could pick up on the subtleties of my voice and learn the nuance of what I was feeling in the car. Brian was like a master chess player: he could out-organize anybody.

Brian, Rick, and I agreed that Brian would take over as team manager. This was a new position in our shop. In years past, Ray had been the crew chief, manager, and czar, and he'd gotten somewhat burned-out. With the new management structure, Brian would manage the team and handle all the big-picture issues, while the crew chief would make the calls relating to the setup of the car and what we did on race day.

Three things had to happen for this new structure to work: the team had to accept two managers in one shop; Brian had to feel comfortable moving out of the spotlight and into a critical but less glamorous managerial role; and we had to find the right guy to fill the role of crew chief.

The first part of the equation didn't seem to be a problem. The team members who stayed did so because they trusted us and believed that we were going to make the right decisions. Plus, it was an opportunity for them. Steve Letarte, one of our tire changers and mechanics, put it best when he said, "I looked at Ray leaving as an opportunity. When you get hired by somebody and work under that regime, as long as the same guy is in charge, you'll always be viewed at the same level no matter how much you've grown. Ray hired me when I was in high school to sweep the floor. It didn't matter how good a mechanic I became or how good a tire changer I could be, he would always look at me as the guy who swept the floor. I think it was a good opportunity for Jeff, too, for the same reasons. When he and Ray started out, he was a nineteen-year-old rookie. It didn't matter that he'd won three championships and fifty races, Ray was still going to look at him as that nineteen-year-old kid. In that regard, the change was good for everybody."

As for Brian, he quickly let everybody know that he wasn't going anywhere. "I'd been around for three championship runs," he told a reporter. "I felt like I'd been a part of building this team from the ground up. I wasn't ready to go back and build another team, especially knowing what Jeff and this team was capable of doing."

A lot of men would have let their egos get the best of them if they had been in Brian's situation. He knew what our new team structure was. He knew he wasn't being demoted. People on the outside did not. It's a heady thing to have your face on national television, to attend press conferences, and see your name and picture in the sports pages. It takes a selfless, mature, and confident person to look objectively at a situation and say, "You know what, I'm good at what I do, but I'm not the man for this job." That was Brian Whitesell.

The final piece of the puzzle was the crew chief. The only way for this system to work was to find somebody with a wealth of experience and a winning attitude who was willing to check his ego at the door. This person had to know that Rick and I were the guys in charge, but he also had to feel comfortable speaking his mind when he put on his headset and keyed his mike. It would take a special personality to fit that bill. We set the bar pretty high. I just hoped the person we envisioned existed somewhere.

Fortunately, he did, and Rick and I found him pretty quickly.

– – – – –

Our list of candidates was short. At the top of that list was a name I kept coming back to: Robbie Loomis. Not only did Rick think he was the kind of guy we were looking for, Ray had actually recommended Robbie. Not long before he left, Ray pulled me aside and said, "You know, you're going to need a good crew chief. I think you should talk to Robbie Loomis over at Petty. He's a good man who knows his stuff."

Ray was particular when it came to praising another crew chief, so I paid attention. Robbie Loomis was a quiet, unassuming crew chief who had grown up in Florida racing in the Thunderbird Division around New Smyrna Beach Speedway until the money ran out. "Then I started working on cars," Robbie said. While he was in high school, he'd worked for an Orlando engine builder named Bo Laws, a legend in Florida racing circles. After bouncing around a few more racing jobs, Robbie's big break came in 1988 when Petty Enterprises hired him as a general mechanic.

Robbie flourished with the Pettys because, like them, he was a solid citizen with high morals, high standards, and a quiet humility that masked a burning desire to win. When Richard Petty launched his two-year farewell tour beginning in 1991, Robbie was The King's crew chief. That spoke volumes for him in my book. Richard Petty was as fine a driver as has ever climbed into a racecar, and he was also a demanding perfectionist. Richard had seen something in Robbie, and his efforts at Petty had impressed me as well.

Robbie and I had first become aware of each other during those seasons he worked with Richard. "The first time I ever saw

Jeff, he started on the outside front row of a Busch race in Rockingham," Robbie said later. "I remember everybody talking about what a hotshot he was because he'd been running so good. I told Dale Inman that day, 'That guy on the front row is going to be tough.' At the time I barely knew Jeff's name. But I kept up with him after that."

My first Winston Cup race at Atlanta in 1992 was Richard's last race. Robbie became crew chief for Rick Wilson and Wally Dallenbach at Petty Enterprises. He also worked with Bobby Hamilton in 1996. After that, Robbie became team manager of Petty Enterprises and the crew chief for John Andretti.

From everything I'd seen or heard about him, Robbie Loomis had it all. He was smart, savvy, hardworking, steady, and experienced. He was a good crew chief. Now, I needed to see if the two of us had chemistry.

He was also loyal. When I called Robbie's home the day after the Pennzoil 400 at Homestead, I left a simple message: "Robbie, this is Jeff Gordon. I'd like to talk to you as soon as possible. Please give me a call at your convenience."

I was a little anxious about what Robbie might say. Asking someone who had been with Richard Petty for eleven years to jump ship was a tall order. I knew that Dale Earnhardt had recruited Robbie back in 1996 and he'd turned them down. I respected that kind of loyalty. If Robbie turned me down, I would understand, but I would be disappointed. He was our first, best choice.

What I didn't know was what the Pettys were telling him.

"What do you think?" Robbie asked Kyle Petty.

"Daddy will tell you that I'll try anything once," Kyle told him. "I've probably tried a few things I shouldn't have, but if you don't try this thing out, you'll never know."

Then The King piped in. "I took it for granted that you'd always be around. Now, if you were talking to me about ninety-nine percent of the deals you could possibly have, I'd tell you to get out of here and get back to work. But Rick Hendrick is good people.

"This is a real good opportunity for you. Jeff's a winner. It wouldn't matter if he was playing golf or baseball or hockey or driving a racecar, he's a winner. Winners are gonna win, and they're gonna breed winners. You're looking for something that Jeff and I have already found. We've won races. We've won championships. That's what you're searching for. I've always told you that what you needed to find was a twenty-five-year-old Richard Petty. I think you've got that in Jeff."

I was twenty-eight at the time, but who was counting? I've always said I would be happy if someday people said one-hundredth of the nice things about me that they say about Richard Petty. To have Richard say those things about me to a man I was trying to hire away from his organization was overwhelming.

It meant a lot to Robbie as well. "I know the standards Richard uses to judge people," Robbie said. "He doesn't care about how much money you have or how many wins you have. It's character that counts with him, and how good you are to your word. When he said that about Jeff and Rick Hendrick, it was just another reason for me to go."

I was in New York in late November when my cell phone rang. It was Robbie. We talked for several minutes, and I could tell he was on the fence. Finally, I made the best pitch I knew how to make: "Robbie, I'd love to have you come on board with us."

Finally he said, "I'd love to come."

Robbie came on in December, just in time to inherit a wealth of headaches. In addition to having to hire a new over-the-wall crew, Goodyear had changed the makeup of their racing tire over the winter, and Chevrolet had changed the body style of the Monte Carlo for 2000. We had a new chassis on new tires, ones that we hadn't raced.

We were one month away from starting the season at Daytona, forty days before taking our first green flag with a new team and a new car.

We were already behind the curve.

Seven

Running Tenth on a Two-Dollar Part

Hiring and training a new pit crew is a huge undertaking. Not only do you have to find people who know what they're doing, you need a group of guys who can learn to work as a seamless unit and who can be responsive to the calls coming from the crew chief. Just like a quarterback has to work overtime with a new group of receivers to get the timing and routes down, it takes time and a lot of repetitions for a pit crew to gel as a unit. Unfortunately, time and reps were in short supply. Our new guys had to learn on the job, which meant they were under a lot of pressure to shorten their learning curve.

One thing working in our favor was how we structured our pit crew this time around. In the past, the Sunday over-the-wall guys didn't work in the shop during the week; they were hired guns who came in on the weekend and went back to other lives (and in some cases, other professions) during the week. We decided to change that and hire guys from within our organization who wanted to double up as mechanics in the shop and tire changers on the weekends. This bred a level of loyalty and commitment that I don't think we would have found if we had hired a crew from the outside.

Then there was the car. Chevy had come out with a new Monte Carlo for 2000, and those of us who raced Chevrolets were presented with a new racing template early in the 1999 season. That would have been fine if we'd had no staff turnover and no distractions. But we didn't have that luxury. Our team was new, and our crew chief was new to us and to Chevrolets.

The third component was the tires. Goodyear had revamped their racing tires, which doesn't sound like a big deal until you consider that all the feel I get from the car, and all the engineering that goes into the design and setup of our cars, hinge on the consistency, durability, weight, balance, and pressure of the tires. Any deviation in that critical variable could throw our entire program off. Suddenly, all the data we had accumulated from years of running at various tracks had to be recalculated—or scrapped altogether.

Not only were the cars and the tires changing, the entire sport was going through a transition. The shocks and springs teams we were using were stiffer and tighter than ever before. With the new aerodynamics and advanced technologies in the suspensions, that's what produces the fastest laps. We're also becoming a more engineering-driven sport. When Rick Hendrick brought the first full-time engineer into Winston Cup racing, nobody was quite sure what an engineer did in our sport. Now, every team has more than one engineer on staff, and some have as many as five or six. The sport was becoming highly specialized, and it was changing rapidly. The teams that were able to adapt to those changes were the ones that would be competitive.

Finally, there was the communication between the crew chief and the driver. With Robbie, I had no history and no frame of reference. In our first test session at Daytona in January, we tested each other out as much as we tested the cars. I would say, "The car is loose in one, but floating a little bit coming out of two," and Robbie had to translate that into something mechanical, an adjustment in tire pressure, a change in the shocks, or a raising or lowering of the track bar (a rear-suspension bar that's attached to the frame on one side of the car and the axel on the other to keep the rear tires centered), to solve the problem I had described. This was no easy task, especially since I was describing a feeling, and he was attempting to translate that into something he could engineer.

Robbie also had to mold himself into an existing championship team. It wasn't like he was starting from scratch where he could build the shop the way he wanted. We had a lot of proven systems in place. Robbie was great about coming and observing the way we did things. He didn't want to change everything his first day on the job, which I saw as a positive sign. He wanted to lead, but he wanted to fit in as well. I thought that showed a lot of maturity.

Unfortunately, we had a long way to go in terms of building our communications. Every driver describes a car differently. In our first day of testing, I saw a lot of blank expressions on Robbie's face. I know he was trying to stay as cool as possible, but he had to be thinking, "How are we going to communicate?"

Throw in the fact that it took a lot of time for us to get used to the new Monte Carlo body, and it was easy to see how far behind the curve we actually were. We hadn't had time to take the new car to the wind tunnel and test various body positions because we were hiring and training staff. It was frustrating. I knew we were behind, but we were doing the best we could from the position we were in. We had to develop lines of communication and work on our chemistry—not just between Robbie and me, but between the old and new members of the team—while trying to test and adjust to this new car body.

The car had more drag than we'd expected with the body position and setups we were using. About all I could say to the press at the time was "It's good we start out here at Daytona where we have restrictor plates, and it's not as strenuous with the chassis work." As for how Robbie and I were working together one week into the process, I told a small group of reporters (who were watching us closely at our Daytona test to see how we got along), "You can get used to each other here a little more than you could starting out somewhere like Rockingham or Martinsville. Right now we have some unknowns as far as working together, but I feel good about the things we are doing this season, and I feel really good about the cars we're building. Our guys could not have done a better job given everything they've been through. I'm sure we're going to go through some things we're not used to going through, and we'll have to work through those things. But the combination of Robbie Loomis as crew chief and Brian Whitesell as team manager couldn't have worked out any better."

Translation: *I have no idea what's going to happen, and all I can do is be as positive and upbeat as possible to encourage these guys.*

It's easy to say that in hindsight, but at the time I had to watch my words carefully. Not only was the racing press scrutinizing every lap we ran and every move we made, a lot of people on our team and in our shop were watching closely as well. Everybody wanted to see how Robbie and I meshed, and how long it would take for us to get the new cars up to speed.

I was equally anxious to see how this was going to work. When we got to Daytona, for the first time in a lot of years, my stomach was in knots with excitement before I got into the car. After eight years with Ray, my routine, whether it was testing, qualifying, or racing, had been pretty much the same. I wouldn't say it had gotten boring—nothing about driving a racecar at 180 miles per hour is dull—but the routine had become predictable. Now, I was getting in the car with fresh eyes and a new outlook. I had more at stake, more pressure, and more at *risk* than at any other point in my career. People were already saying out loud what they had been whispering for months: that we would be lucky to be a middle-of-the-pack team. I thought people were too quick to judge, and more than anything, I wanted to prove that they were being hasty in their judgment.

"We've been put to the test before," I told a reporter before the start of the Daytona 500. "This is just another test, another challenge. We've never backed away from a challenge. We're not here to prove anything to anybody, and our job is not to make a lot of friends. Our goal is to win races, and win championships."

Then the whole week almost fell apart for us. During happy hour on Saturday afternoon, the day before the biggest race of the NASCAR season, Mike Bliss's car got loose in turn one. To save it, he swerved down onto the apron and in front of a pack of cars. Everybody got out of the gas, but I was too close to avoid Dale Jarrett's car. The hood of my car smashed into the rear end of Dale's, causing serious damage to our primary racecar, the one we hoped to put on the track in less than eighteen hours.

My first thought was that we would go with the backup car. Given the time, energy, and hours we had worked throughout the week, I didn't think we had a chance of getting the primary car ready to race. But Robbie was an optimist. We had been running the fastest laps in the field during happy hour (right before crashing into Dale Jarrett), and Robbie didn't want to take such a fast car out of commission if he didn't have to. He thought we could repair the car and be ready by noon the next day. He asked for my input, which was good. I wanted to be more involved in those kinds of decisions, and Robbie wanted me more involved. I agreed that we should fix the car if we could.

The guys worked all night getting the car ready for Sunday. By the time the green flag fell, they were exhausted, but full of adrenaline. Everybody wanted to see if this gamble had paid off. Regardless of how things worked out, I was proud of their effort.

On the first lap, we dropped from eleventh to fifteenth. My line wasn't the fastest line and I got stuck outside a group of cars that were moving fast on the inside. It's always that way in a re-strictor-plate race. I had to be patient. Finally taking an inside line, I drafted off Dale Earnhardt when he dropped in front of me. We had worked together the year before, and then battled each other to the finish line in the final ten laps of the race. Now I was behind Dale hoping to draft with him long enough for the two of us to work our way up front. On lap 25, Dale and I broke into the top ten and were inching our way toward the leaders.

Five laps later, my quest for a third Daytona 500 title was effectively over.

I took a higher line to gain momentum, which looked like a good decision. Several guys were finding success with a high line, and the car felt better up there. That was when the plume of black smoke started billowing from under my car. "Guys, we've got a problem," I said over the radio.

"Just stay out there," Robbie said. "Let's see what happens."

Two laps later, NASCAR officials made us pit. I knew I had an engine problem, so I pulled off pit road. The crew lifted the hood to survey the damage. From the cockpit I could see the mechanic's shoulders sag. The good news was that the problem was a broken oil fitting, an easy piece to replace. We would be able to finish the race. The bad news was that we had been forced to sit in the pit for over seven minutes. We had lost any chance of contending for the title because of a two-dollar part. When I got back out on the track, we were four laps down and running in forty-third place.

Dale Jarrett won his third Daytona 500 that afternoon. I finished thirty-fourth.

– – – – –

Daytona was a tough day for me, and even tougher for Robbie. When we went up in smoke, a throng of fans stood up and cheered. Later I heard Robbie say, "Man, this is the worst day of my life, and we've got two hundred thousand people who think it's great!"

We didn't talk much that afternoon. I was disappointed, especially given how meticulously we had prepared for this race only to have it fall apart because of something as minor as an oil fitting. I didn't blame Robbie. It could just as easily have happened to any other crew chief. But that didn't make the pill any easier to swallow. You build and work all winter with one race in mind: the Daytona 500. That only adds to the pressure. We had come into the biggest race of the year under a microscope, and we'd given our critics something to talk about.

A week later in Rockingham we qualified fifth and seemed to have arrived with a good car and a good attitude. Early in the race I found the line I liked and I pushed the car into third place. We fell back after our tires got hot, but after another good yellow-flag pit stop, we worked our way back up to seventh place. By lap 119, I was in fifth place, and by lap 187, I had the lead. We led for sixteen laps before a yellow flag brought everyone into the pits. We took four tires and topped off the fuel in a fourteen-second stop. It was early, but we seemed to have come out with more fire, as if Daytona had ignited our competitive juices. When the jack fell and all four wheels touched the ground, I sped out of the pit. We hadn't lost our lead. If I could get a good jump off the restart, we had a chance to put some distance between our car and the rest of the field.

When the track went green, I felt a vibrating on the right side of the car like the tire was flat. But I knew it wasn't a flat. It was worse than a flat. A flat is something that happens out of the blue, something you don't like, and something you do your best to avoid through testing and careful inspection of every tire, but you know there will be times when it's going to happen. You're running well, and all of a sudden you feel the car loosen as the tire goes. You hate it, but it's one of those bad-luck facts of racing. We didn't have a flat. We had a loose tire, a tire that hadn't been tightened during the pit stop. The tire itself was fine. The car was running great. But the team had missed two lug nuts. The distinct vibration I was feeling could only be from a loose wheel. We would have to pit under green and relinquish our lead. I tried not to let disappointment slip into my voice, but I'm sure Robbie sensed my frustration.

"It's times like those you want to crawl into a hole and disappear," Robbie said later. "You can hear it in your driver's voice and see it in his eyes. We let him down."

We came back and finished tenth, but it wasn't a happy finish.

Robbie called me at home that night, and I could hear the despair in his voice. "Look," Robbie said after apologizing. "This thing's going to take some time. We've got new guys, I'm new working with you, we've got some work to do on the car; we're going to have to work our way through some tough times. We might have to run tenth for a while. It's not the end of the world. You've enjoyed great success, and we can enjoy that success again soon if we just have some time."

"I understand," I told him. "This is a process. It's early. I don't like it, but I know you don't like it either. I also know we'll get there."

I understood that this was a process, and it would, indeed, take time to rebuild. I also knew that Robbie and this new team needed to see me and hear my assurances. It wasn't enough for me to chat with the crew chief and go my own way. Robbie needed a lot of support, and I believed in him. I had to play a larger role. I had to face the realities of my new position. This was where I had to jump in and make a difference.

Robbie suggested that I start holding team meetings. I thought that was a great idea.

"Okay," he said. "When?"

"Next week. We need to get together before the race for a few minutes. Nothing major. I'm not going to undermine your authority. I just need the rest of the team to hear what I'm telling you."

"What's that?"

"That you are my guy, and we're in this for the long haul."

The next Sunday in Las Vegas, we had a two-minute team meeting in the transporter moments before driver introductions. "Guys," I said, "we've had a tough couple of weeks. I don't like running the way we've run, but we can handle having bad runs from time to time as long as we continue making steady progress. We didn't become a championship team in two weeks, and we haven't lost our edge in two weeks either. I want you to know that I'm with you. You are my team. Robbie and Brian are my guys. We're in this together."

I don't know if the words sank in, but I think the fact that I was calling a meeting was a message they got loud and clear. The meetings would become a weekly ritual. Win or lose, this was my team now.

I just hoped we didn't keep losing for long. Unfortunately, we gave our critics more ammunition after that first meeting. We had qualified tenth, a fair start from a spot where I thought we had a chance, but as soon as the race started, we fell back. Cars passed me like I was standing still. Before I could figure out what we needed to fix, we were in twentieth place and going backward. I brought the car back to the pits, but it was no use. We came in and made major adjustments to the car, which I'm certain would have made it better, but we didn't get a chance to try them out. Rain washed out the rest of the race. We finished a grim twenty-eighth.

It was a long, quiet trip home that night.

I knew I had to take the long view of this process, and I had to convey that same message to Robbie and the team. It would be tough, but I could live with tough as long as we kept moving in the right direction.

I reinforced that message in our second team meeting in Atlanta a week later. "I'm with you," I said. I knew I was repeating myself, but we needed all the positive reinforcement we could get. "I want to win, but more than anything I want us to improve, get better every week, and learn from each other. We're going to have some tough times, but tough times make us stronger and bring us closer together."

More nods from the guys. They were starting to get the message. I was with them, but we needed to make progress.

After a prayer and a team chant, the crew walked single file out the back of the transporter. I grabbed Robbie by the shirtsleeve.

"Yeah, Bud," he said.

"You know I believe in you," I told him.

"I know."

"You remember what you told me that night after Rockingham, about running tenth for a while?"

"Sure I do."

"I agree with you," I said. "But, I don't believe we're going to run down there very long. I believe we're going to turn this thing around quicker than anybody expected."

He smiled and nodded. I hoped my encouragement was helping.

That afternoon we finished ninth. A week later in Darlington, we finished eighth, and in Bristol, we posted another eighth-place finish. Three top tens in three weeks didn't set any records, but it was the kind of steady improvement we needed.

– – – – –

In 2000, we were nonfactors in the dozen races held in California, Indianapolis, Pocono, Michigan, Dover, Daytona, and New Hampshire, all tracks where I'd performed well throughout the years, and where I had racked up eighteen career wins. We won in April in a restrictor-plate race at Talladega, which was a great boost for our confidence. Your first win of the year is always huge. Given the pressure and scrutiny we were under, our first win that year was like a weight being lifted from our shoulders. It didn't do a lot for us in terms of the points standings, but it was like a bolt of lightning to our confidence. Another win in June at Sears Point gave us a second shot of morale at just the right time. We certainly needed it.

Through twenty races, we had only led a total of 347 laps, the lowest number since my rookie year. Robbie and I were beginning to communicate better, but our finishes weren't up to par. It took longer than we had hoped to work through all the aerodynamic issues of the new Monte Carlo. For the first few months we just hadn't figured it out. Chevrolet and our engineering and fabrication staff bent over backward to help. They sent teams of engineers to work through the problems. By midsummer we started to see results. After our win at Sears Point we had a tenth-place finish at Daytona in the Pepsi 400, and two top fives in New Hampshire and Pocono.

It also took longer for the team to click. At the top level of any sport, the slightest change in the makeup of a team can have an adverse effect. Knock Brett Favre out for the season and the Packers will still be a good team, but they won't be the same kind of good they were with Brett in the lineup. We had switched out almost every position. The people we had from the old team were in new jobs, and the new guys were still learning. People who expected us to come out and win a lot of races right off the bat either didn't know our sport or they were fooling themselves. Bobby Labonte, who led the points race for most of the 2000 season, did so with a veteran team. They were a finely tuned unit, while we were a group of talented, hard-working guys who had been together a grand total of six months.

At times in the first half of the year, Robbie would look at Brian with a confused gaze in his eyes, and Brian would shrug his shoulders. The other team members saw this. They knew what was happening. This was a process. Every time we had a communications breakdown, even if the car was still running, it planted a seed of doubt. I could give all the prerace speeches I wanted, but if we didn't start performing, it wouldn't make any difference.

Thankfully, our communication got better with each passing week. As Robbie and I grew closer, I realized that we were much more alike in our personalities than Ray and I had ever been. Robbie was steady, even-keeled, good-natured, hilariously dry-witted, extremely competitive, and willing to give everyone around him a chance to prove himself as long as the talent and effort was there. He might tell a joke and ask about a team member's family as he strolled through the garage. By midsummer, I was happy to have found someone who was more like me, but I also worried that we still hadn't found a winning rhythm.

My personal low point of that year came in August. It seemed that when we needed a break, bad luck followed us like a curse. At the Brickyard 400 in Indianapolis, twenty miles from where I'd grown up, I got caught up in an early accident. It didn't knock us out, but it might as well have. We finished thirty-third, two laps down.

A week later at Watkins Glen, one of two road courses we race during the year, I was looking to extend my streak of consecutive road-course wins (I had won the last six, including our early 2000 victory at Sears Point). I already held the record for consecutive road-course wins, and I was tied with Richard Petty,

Bobby Allison, and Rusty Wallace for the all-time road-course record with six. A win at Watkins Glen would take the record outright, but given where we were, a win of any kind would have been a blessing.

It didn't take long for those ideas to fade to black. On lap two, Tony Stewart and I were side by side going two-wide into the S curves, which is something that will not work at that track. I was forced into the guardrail. The steering was knocked out of whack, and the track bar was rubbing against the fuel cell. The team did what they could to bend the fender off the tire and get us back out, but we lost a lap. In road-course racing, that pretty much ends your day. We finished twenty-third.

A week later in Michigan, I found myself too close to Tony Stewart again. I've always liked Tony and considered him one of those drivers who got a bad rap. We never met prior to racing in Winston Cup together, even though we both came up in open-wheel racing. I do recall someone telling me once that if I stayed in midget racing, I was going to have some tough competition from an up-and-coming kid named Tony Stewart, but our paths never crossed. When we did met, I thought he was a great guy—funny, friendly, talented, everything you'd want from a fellow competitor. There have been times when he's had conflicts with the media. He's an intense competitor, and that intensity has put him in conflict with some reporters. Hopefully fans see him for the nice guy that he is.

As nice as I think Tony is, I wasn't thrilled when he spun out in front of me in Michigan. While I missed hitting him head-on, Tony's car clipped my front left fender and I brushed the wall on the right. We limped in with a thirty-sixth-place finish.

We closed out August with a twenty-third-place finish at

Bristol, which was our best finish of the month. That prompted another visit from Robbie, this time in my motor home during a rain delay. "I know we're not showing it, but I think we're really close," he said. "You might think I'm crazy, but I believe if we'd caught a couple of breaks, we would be right there."

"I don't think you're crazy," I said. "I agree with you."

I could tell that surprised him.

"Look," I said. "I've been racing my whole life, and I've won a lot. But as much as I've won, I've lost a lot more. Losing is inevitable. You don't have to like it—I sure don't—but you have to accept it as a fact of life. We've gotten better in the last month. I know it, and you know it. The only thing we have to do is keep the team excited and believing in themselves."

This was easier said than done. The whispers about us being "done" were a full-throated chorus now. The abuse Robbie took was brutal. Every local paper in every town we went to ran stories that led with "What's wrong with Jeff Gordon?" Every week I answered the same way: "Nothing. We're a young team, a new team. We're in a new car, and we're learning. We're getting better every week, and we're not far from having it."

Before the fall race at Darlington, I told the media, "I've been really happy with how we've been running lately." The reporters squinted and gave me that "Come on, who are you kidding?" look. "No, really," I insisted. "You've just got to get it all together. You've got to get all that karma and chemistry it takes to win working at the same time. I was talking to Benny Parsons, and he said, 'The law of averages has caught up with you.' I said, 'I knew it was coming. I knew it would happen eventually. I just hope we don't stay on this average much longer and we get back to those other averages.' "

Whether that group of reporters believed me, I don't know. That message was for my fans, and more importantly, for my team. They needed to see me supporting them as strongly in public as I did in our team meetings. By the time they saw me make my supporting statements in Darlington, statements they'd heard for the umpteenth time by the first of September, I knew they believed me. I could see it in their eyes.

That weekend we qualified tenth and finished fourth, our first top five in more than a month. It wasn't Victory Lane, but it was the start of something special. I felt something that afternoon, something in the chemistry in our trailer and in the mood at the team meeting; something in the way the guys responded to Robbie and the way Robbie responded to me. The karma might not have come completely our way that day, but we had definitely made a turn.

For the first time all season, I no longer thought, "We're close." I thought, "We're real, real close."

— — — — —

We had grilled chicken the following Saturday. Every team has someone on-site who prepares meals, usually on a grill just outside the transporter. Teams come in from a busy morning of last-minute preparations, and they have a buffet spread out on one of the cabinets in their hauler. It's not Spago, but the competition between those outdoor chefs can get pretty intense, especially when one driver or crew chief starts bragging about the meals he's getting on race day. This week, Mary cooked chicken with peppers and onions. It was one of the few times in the season she got to cook dinner, and one of the only times she did so for a Saturday-night race.

Everybody's schedule was a little out of sync. The Chevrolet Monte Carlo 400 at Richmond International Raceway was one of a few Saturday-night races we ran in 2000, so we had to readjust our rhythm. It wasn't a huge deal, especially since everybody else in the field had to make the same adjustments, but we still felt it.

Another difference was the vibrancy I felt from our team in the moments leading up to driver introductions. Our front tire carrier, Craig Curione, and Shane Church, our rear tire changer, were debating the merits of Kid Rock's first album, while Robbie and Brian were going over the setup sheets one last time. There was electricity in our transporter that evening, a buzz of positive energy that I hadn't felt in a long time. When I called the team together for our prerace meeting, I told them, "It's been a long, tough season, but I feel great about where we are this week. I've got a feeling we're back on track. Now, let's go have some fun and see if we can win one."

Richmond is a short track (three-quarters of a mile) where a lot can happen. Everybody expects a lot of lead changes, and a lot of late-race strategic decisions. This was no exception. Jeff Burton, who won the pole with a track record of 125.78 miles per hour, kept the lead for the first eighty-nine laps of the race. Then Rusty Wallace jumped ahead for eighty-six laps. When Rusty's motor dropped a cylinder, Tony Stewart took the lead.

We started the race as the fifteenth-fastest car, and that's where we stayed through most of the first half of the race. Fortunately, we avoided the nasty crashes that took out six cars. With forty laps remaining, we had worked into the top five, but it would take a little luck and some quick thinking for us to have a chance. Bobby Labonte, who had led the points race all but three weeks of the season, had the fastest car. Good things would have to happen to us if the tide was going to turn.

We caught our first break when Bobby had problems. When the sixth caution of the night came out with forty laps to go, Bobby got in and out of the pits quickly and fell in line behind the leader, Steve Park. If things had worked out, I figured Bobby would have passed Steve on the restart, and the rest of the night would have been a race for second place. But Bobby broke a steering pump either during the pit stop or during his first caution lap after getting back out. He had to pit again and ran the rest of the race without power steering, finishing fifteenth, one lap down.

When the track went green, Jeff Burton took the lead from Steve Park. I fell in behind Jeff to get by Steve as well. It looked like we would finish one and two, with Jeff winning by more than second. Then we caught our second big break of the night. Casey Atwood blew an engine with less than twenty laps to go, bringing out the seventh caution.

"Stay out there, Bud," Robbie said.

"Got it," I said. This was a great call. We were in a fifteen-lap shoot-out with only a dozen cars on the lead lap. The tires were good enough to make it, and I thought the car was good enough to get past Jeff Burton on a restart. The only question was how good the guys who pitted would be with fresh tires.

"We're going green next time by," Ron Thiel said. We were going green on the next lap. Although he tried to hide it, I could hear the excitement in Ron's voice. This one was going to be close.

I backed off of Jeff's rear just far enough to get a good run. You don't really enter a restart with a plan. If Jeff went low, I would go high. If he went high, I would try to slip below him. He didn't know which way I would go either, so it was a game of who could react the fastest to what the other was doing. When I heard the call—"Green, green, green"—I saw Jeff make a slight move to protect the inside. That was all I needed. I pointed the nose of the car high and powered around the right side of Jeff's car to take our first lead of the night.

It looked like smooth sailing for a couple of laps. Then I looked in my mirror and saw a sight that made my heart pick up a beat or two. The black car of Dale Earnhardt looked like it had been shot out of a cannon as it came up behind me. Dale and Mark Martin were two of the drivers who'd pitted. They had fresh tires and a lot of momentum as they made a run at my lead.

Our final break came when it took Dale three laps to get past Steve Park, who did a great job of blocking even though Dale clearly had the fastest car. When Dale finally passed Steve, he charged behind me. Fortunately, I saw the white flag and heard Robbie saying the words I wanted to hear: "One to go."

I held off Dale by three-quarters of a second. It wasn't the biggest win of my career or the most lucrative or the most exciting or prestigious. It was just one of the most important. That was the night I felt our momentum changing. All the things lined up for us, and everything had gone our way.

After Richmond I knew it for sure: we were back.

The next day NASCAR penalized us for an improper intake manifold during our Richmond victory. Some people (race reporters among them) thought that tainted our win; what it really did was fire us up and make us want to work that much harder. It had been a long, tough road, one that could have run us into a ditch if we had let the negativity get to us. Our guys fought, clawed, sweated, cried, and did what it took to make us winners again. We left Richmond that night seven hundred points out of the lead, and out of the Winston Cup championship race. But we had our swagger back. And everybody knew it.

– – – – –

In the last eleven races of 2000 we finished in the top nine ten times and would have made it eleven for eleven but we got caught up in a crash that involved Rusty Wallace and Dale Jarrett in Charlotte after we'd won the pole. We were thirty-ninth that day, but in ten out of the last eleven races our average finish was 4.9 with two poles (our second came in Atlanta in the last race of the year). That was an unbelievable finish, one I was extremely proud of for our team.

You had to search long and hard for good news from our 2000 season, but those last eleven races convinced me that we would be championship contenders again in 2001. A lot of people had written us off; a lot more said it would take three or four years for us to get back on track. Not everybody was paying attention when we finished fourth in Atlanta to finish the year 769 points behind Bobby Labonte, but I knew we had crossed a threshold. This team had had to overcome a lot, and they had come through it stronger and better than any other I'd ever seen. I couldn't wait to get to Daytona in January for testing.

In December I attended the NASCAR banquet in New York as I had every year since I'd started in Winston Cup racing. Only this year I wasn't seated at the head table or anywhere near the front of the room. The ninth-place table was in a corner next to a giant speaker that looked like it had been stolen from Tommy Lee's basement. As the program got under way, the sound was so loud I felt it in my chest.

I leaned over to Rick and yelled, "I don't want to . . ."

"What?" Rick yelled back.

"I said, I don't want to ever sit here again. Next year we're going to be at the head table."

Eight

Daytona

ew fans to our sport (and there are plenty of those) often wonder why our biggest race is at the beginning of the season instead of the end. We don't have a play-off system like team sports. Every week, forty-three Winston Cup drivers compete head-to-head. The championship is determined at the end of the year based on total points. But our grand event, our Super Bowl, is always the first race of the year in February: the Daytona 500. The history of this race goes back almost seventy years.

I've read and heard over the years that stockcar racing began in Georgia when a group of moonshiners carved a quarter-mile track in a cow pasture and bet a case of corn liquor on who had the fastest car. Legend has it that the drivers came from the back roads of North Carolina, Tennessee, Alabama, Georgia, and Kentucky, men who had learned to avoid tax men (called revenuers) who sought to arrest them for not paying taxes on their "shine." As a result, stockcar racing earned an outlaw reputation that would remain a part of the sport for the better part of a half century.

Then a gas station owner in Florida decided to turn this group of renegade bootleg runners into a sporting franchise.

Bill France Sr. moved his family to Florida from Maryland during the Depression. He thought he could find work in Miami, which is where he was headed when he stumbled across the little beach town of Daytona. It wasn't much of a town, a few businesses near a long, straight stretch of hard, brown beach. But it was the beach that attracted Big Bill.

The story goes that the five-hundred-yard-wide, brick-hard

sand attracted racecar drivers from all over the world. Big Bill loved cars, so he got a job as a painter in Daytona until he earned enough money to buy a local gas station. In the twenties and early thirties, the twenty-mile stretch of Daytona shoreline was used to set land speed records, and the events always drew huge crowds. Those land speed attempts became the main event at something locals called Speedweek. A stockcar race on the beach was one of the side attractions.

Unfortunately, when the Atlantic headwinds kept Sir Malcolm Campbell from breaking the 275-mile-per-hour mark in 1935, land speed drivers moved to Utah and the Bonneville Salt Flats. Panicked locals approached Bill France in the hopes that he could somehow keep the beach race alive. Big Bill and a local restaurant owner named Charlie Reece signed on to sponsor the race. The two of them put on a heck of a show in 1936. Bill charged fifty cents for spectators to see the July Fourth extravaganza. He gave a bottle of rum to each lap leader, a case of Pennzoil motor oil for winning the pole, and a box of Hav-A-Tampa cigars for showing up sober at the drivers' meeting. He set rules: the doors and hoods would be bolted shut, and the top five cars would be inspected after the race before any prize money was given out to avoid any shenanigans.

The race was a huge success. Big Bill was in the racing business.

In 1948, after turning the Daytona race into a bigger event than it had ever been, and expanding his races to include the 100-Mile National Championship race on a dirt track he'd rented in Charlotte, Bill France formed the National Association for Stock Car Auto Racing, NASCAR. Ten years later he risked the fortune he had amassed with his new league to take his sport off the dirt tracks and onto the next level. On a parcel of land nobody but the bears, snakes, and Florida panthers wanted, Bill France built the Daytona International Speedway and launched the Granddaddy of Them All, the Daytona 500, in 1959.

Forty-two thousand fans came to witness the first Daytona 500. They saw a doozy. After five hundred miles, Lee Petty and John Beauchamp were so close at the finish that nobody could tell who won the race. Big Bill announced that Beauchamp was the "unofficial" winner until still photos and movies proved that Lee Petty crossed the finish line first by no more than a couple of feet.

Lee Petty (Richard's father) told reporters afterward, "If you can't write about this, you can't write about nothing."

The next year, over seventy thousand people showed up to watch the Daytona 500. From that moment on, it was the biggest event in stockcar racing, our Super Bowl, World Series, and Grand Slam rolled into one.

— — — — —

Winning the Daytona 500 twice before my thirtieth birthday was one of my greatest accomplishments in racing. But I wasn't thinking about past wins when we arrived at Daytona in the warm, windy February of 2001. We had tested well in January, and I felt more comfortable going into the season than I had since we'd won thirteen races in 1998. The struggles we'd gone through in 1999 and 2000 had brought our team closer together and forced me to become a more mature leader. Now I hoped to reap the fruits of our efforts. I knew we were in great shape to contend for the championship, but we still had to perform on the track. You have to have all the right ingredients.

We looked strong early, running seventh fastest in the first practice session with a speed of 181.441. The car slowed down a fraction in the afternoon (181.280 mph), but we were still a top-ten performer going into qualifying.

The Daytona 500 is a little different from other races in that we qualify a week before the race rather than a day or two ahead of time. From the time we qualify until the actual race, we run in several other events including the Twin 125, and the Budweiser Shootout, both nonpoint events that have become a traditional part of Speedweek. I look at all the races as important, but the 500 is the big event. I wanted to qualify well to get our momentum rolling.

We went out late—forty-ninth out of fifty-two cars—which I viewed as a plus. I like knowing how fast I need to run. At the time of our run, Bill Elliott had the fastest time, but my teammate Jerry Nadeau was in second. Since Jerry's car and engine came out of the same shop as ours, and we knew everything about Jerry's setup, I felt good about our chances.

One lap in I knew we had a fast car, but I wasn't sure it was fast enough. Daytona International Speedway is a tri-oval (imagine rounding the corners of a triangle) with thirty-one degrees of banking in the turns, eighteen degrees of banking in the tri-oval frontstretch, and three degrees of banking in the backstretch. To qualify well you need to run a high line on your first lap to build momentum, then run a low lap the second time around for speed. When I crossed the start-finish line, I had a lap time of 49.666 seconds. That equated to 181.210 miles per hour, not good enough to win the pole, but the thirteenth-fastest time in the field. After qualifying, NASCAR officials determined that one of the cars ahead of us had fudged the rules a little. The roof of the 25 car measured a half inch low in postqualifying inspection, which meant their time was disallowed and we moved up to twelfth, a good spot, especially in a restrictor-plate race.

You have to have help at Daytona, a point I made during my postqualifying press conference. "You've got to have somebody to go with you," I told the group of reporters. "If you're out in front, you can only hope that the guy behind you doesn't have any [drafting] help.

"You just don't know how this race is going to turn out."

I had no idea how prophetic those words would turn out to be.

– – – – –

Any lead at Daytona is a good lead, but the best lead is the one you have going into turn four on the final lap. Any other time, even with only one lap to go, you're a target. Two or three guys who have hooked up as partners are probably going to get by you.

We were able to maneuver through the pack pretty good once the race got under way. As the track heated up, we made some minor adjustments in tire pressure, which seemed to work well. On lap 107, I worked my way into the lead and held that top spot for four laps. I lost the lead just as quickly. No lead is safe at Daytona. It's like running in the *peloton* in the Tour de France, except there's no Lance Armstrong pulling away from the field. It's hard to get enough momentum on that track to get around the leaders. Numbers work to your advantage as long as everybody stays upright and on the pavement. It's when that first guy falls (or in our case, crashes) that the problems arise.

I was able to move up front a few more times throughout the race, leading laps 116 through 119 before being overtaken, and regaining the lead again twenty laps later for three laps. So far we'd enjoyed a good run. The car was responding well to the adjustments we were making. Robbie and Brian had put together a good setup package for the day. Unfortunately, in restrictor-plate racing, I don't have a lot of friends out there working with me. I don't know why, but I have a hard time finding "buddies" when it comes to drafting. I fell in with whomever I could get behind, as I usually did on this track, and waited to make a move. The trick was avoiding the Big One, the crash we all knew was probably coming, but hoped we could avoid. You can't run that many cars that close together at those speeds without a slipup somewhere along the way. When that happens, it's like a rush-hour pileup at 180 miles per hour.

Our luck ran out on lap 174. Robby Gordon tried to squeeze through a hole that wasn't big enough, and his front fender clipped Ward Burton. Ward got loose from the contact. When he tried to recover, he slid into Tony Stewart. Tony had no chance of missing this wreck. I was back in the pack, so I couldn't pick up on exactly what had happened, but when I saw Tony's orange car get airborne, I knew this was going to be a big one.

This was one of those spectacular crashes that make all the evening highlight reels, the kind you expect to see in a Jerry Bruckheimer movie. Tony's car spun, air got underneath his chassis, and the rear end of the car went flying up. Once the rear

The banner introducing us as the 1995 Winston Cup champions was a source of pride for everyone on our team. *Chobat Racing Images*

1998
NASCAR
Winston Cup
Champion

Brian Whitesell did an outstanding job as our interim crew chief. Here we are after our first win together—it's hard to tell who's happier. *CIA Stock Photo*

Not too long ago, I was considered the "young gun" in NASCAR. Now it's guys like my teammate, Jimmie Johnson (right), who own that title. *C. Scott McNair, MD*

Left: Our crowning moment: Ray Evernham and I hoist what would turn out to be our last Winston Cup Championship trophy together. We won thirteen races that year. *Courtesy of Patrick Dorsey, 1998*

In my opinion, Rick Hendrick is the best team owner in racing. *AP Wide World Photos*

It took some time for Robbie Loomis and me to develop our communications, but our temperaments and personalities have always fit together perfectly. *CIA Stock Photo*

Every win is sweet, but capturing the 2001 Winston Cup Championship was about as good as it got for Robbie and me. *Chobat Racing Images*

Previous page: Only in America could a kid from a working-class California family do the things I've been able to do. *CIA Stock Photo*

wheels left the ground, it was all over. Tony flipped twice, spun twice, and landed on his teammate, Bobby Labonte. This ended up being a nineteen-car wreck.

After Tony's car got airborne, all I saw was white smoke. I tried to dive low to get around the mess, but that was wishful thinking. I hit a car in front of me and was hit by a car behind me. I spun; I braked; I did what I could to avoid any further damage, but it was no use. This was one of those times when I had no chance. Wrong place, wrong time, and you're in the Big One.

I've always viewed crashes as being like falling off a horse. If you ride long enough, it's going to happen. If you race cars for long enough, you're going to be in some wrecks; they're as unavoidable as rain. But just as a jockey has to get back on his horse, a driver has to get back in the racecar after a crash. If he doesn't, the wreck could have a long-term effect on his confidence.

I can tell you every detail of every crash I've ever been in going back to the days when I was a kid racing go-karts. There was the time when Paul McMahan and I got tangled up and drove into the hay bales at Capital quarter-midget track. I think I was seven years old at the time. Then there was the end-over-end crash in a sprinter at the Tri-State Speedway in Indiana when I was sixteen. In 1991 I had an ugly one at the USAC Four Crown Nationals. Later that year I totaled a Toyota racing truck I was testing, and I've been in numerous bang-ups in midgets, Busch cars, and Winston Cup racing. I remember every one and can walk anyone who asks me about them through every detail.

The first feeling is helplessness. You see what's happening, but you know that once you get caught up in the wreck, there's nothing you can do about it. It's like all the adrenaline that's been running through your veins evaporates immediately. All of a sudden, after being focused all day on going as fast as you can, you're stuck going nowhere. It's like having your legs cut out from under you; you want to keep running, but you can't.

Then you get angry. There's a reason drivers who are interviewed minutes after they've crashed often have harsh words for whoever they believe caused the wreck. I try not to vent in front of any cameras, but I'm angry when I wreck, and at times when I've gotten caught up in a crash, people listening on the scanners have got an earful. It's not until you have a few minutes to decompress that you start thinking about what happened, and what you might have done to avoid the wreck.

I never obsess over my crashes—I don't think about them at all unless I'm asked—but I do remember them. Maybe the reason I have no trouble recalling my wrecks and I'm not inhibited about discussing them is because, with the exception of some bruised ribs from a 1999 crash in Texas, I've never been seriously injured. The closest I've come to being sidelined because of a wreck came in 2002 in a golf cart race. We were in Richmond doing a Warner Brothers' promotion with the Looney Tunes characters. I had Bugs Bunny on the back of my golf cart, and I was leading the race (Jimmie Johnson was a close second). When I made a turn, the seat of the golf cart was so slick that I slid off and hit the pavement hard, bruising my ribs, injuring my hand, and crushing every ounce of dignity I had left. Film of that one made it to every network and was the teaser for every *Sports Center* telecast for a couple of days. Worse than the pain was the embarrassment, but it hurt plenty.

I don't mind talking about my crashes, because it's a part of racing, but I don't ponder them. If I've done something wrong that causes a crash, I analyze that mistake, work through what I should have done differently, and chalk it up to experience. What I won't do is replay a crash over and over in my mind. I've always believed that if you think about crashes, you're going to crash. If you think about winning, you're going to win. When I'm in the car, I think about winning. Everything else takes a mental backseat.

I've also never believed NASCAR viewers tune in just to see the crashes, just as I don't believe hockey fans watch the Stanley Cup finals for the fights. There might be a few fans who enjoy watching guys spin out, hit each other, or slide into the walls, but they are in the minority. Although I have to admit that crashes might pique the curiosity of some who have never seen a NASCAR race and cause them to tune in for the first time, everybody wants to see the drivers get up and walk away. It's not a calling card any of us like to leave, but you won't find a driver in the garage who won't acknowledge that crashes draw interest to the sport.

In 1979, a crash propelled our sport into the national spotlight and elevated the Daytona 500 to a new level. According to what I've read, this was the first time the race had been televised live, a big risk for CBS since most programming executives thought NASCAR was a regional sport with little or no national audience. Fortunately, much of the Northeast and the Midwest had been blanketed by a blizzard, which kept folks indoors and glued to whatever happened to be on television. A record television audience saw Donnie Allison lead Cale Yarborough into the final lap by mere inches. It was a two-man race. Richard Petty was nineteen seconds behind.

Halfway down the back straightaway, Cale made a move to the inside. Donnie went low to block him, and when he did, the two bumped. Cale slide low into the grass between the track and Lake Lloyd, a small infield pond. Cale came back onto the track, and there was more contact.

Richard was so far back he didn't even see the crash, but he cruised to victory by a car length over Darrell Waltrip.

About the time Richard took the checkered flag, CBS commentator Ken Squier squealed, "There's a fight in turn three!" When the cameras turned back to the track, they caught Cale in the middle of a fistfight with Donnie Allison and his brother Bobby, who had stopped to lend a hand. The spectacle was talked about for years to come and shined a spotlight on our sport. Suddenly, NASCAR wasn't just a bunch of cars going in circles: it was a human sport where passions ran high. Too bad it took a crash and a fistfight for people to notice.

– – – – –

Tony's crash in 2001 looked a lot worse than it was. Anytime a car is tumbling or spinning, it's slowing down. The bad-looking crashes are usually the ones people walk away from. It's those that don't look dramatic that can be bad. In the case of a car like Tony's that was flipping through the air, the driver is getting thrown around, and he'll probably tell you later that it was a real bad wreck, but he's also harnessed in tightly and protected by the best safety equipment available. Tony's crash looked horrible because the car was flipping through the air with parts flying in all directions. Every part that flew off the car absorbed energy, and every tumble slowed the momentum. Tony might be bruised, sore, or have a cracked rib or two, but he should be okay.

The rest of us were uninjured, just out of the race.

I kept my head down as I made the walk back through the infield. We had had a good car and were on our way to a solid finish. Now we would start the year with a DNF and have to work our way out of a hole. After a visit to the infield medical center (where I was checked and released in about a minute), I went back to our transporter, where I changed clothes in the lounge and watched the rest of the race on television.

Fox was televising Winston Cup racing for the first time, and they were doing a heck of a good job. Rupert Murdoch had spent over a billion dollars for the right to televise the first half of the next six seasons, with the Daytona 500 as the biggest jewel in that sporting crown. The network hired Darrell Waltrip to provide commentary, and from what I'd seen he was very entertaining. They taped every event during Speedweek to work out the production bugs, and I was impressed by what they were doing. Not only were Darrell's comments insightful, the quality of the production was great. They had cameras at eye level through the turns, and tracking devices that showed the viewer what cars were in the lead. The problem with past productions was that speed didn't translate well to a two-dimensional television screen. Someone at home couldn't tell if we were going 70 or 170, and the shots from the blimp made us look like two-inch slot cars. Fox hadn't solved all those problems, but they had gone a long way to improve the viewing experience. When I looked up at the screen in the transporter, my first thought was "This is impressive."

Dale Earnhardt had just missed getting caught up in the Big

One along with the rest of us. He was low on the track and less than a car length ahead of Tony when things went haywire, and he slid by unscathed. When the track went green after the cleanup, two Earnhardts were out in front. Dale Jr. led with his father right behind him. One lap later, Michael Waltrip, another of Dale's drivers, passed the Intimidator to take over second place. I could tell the DEI cars were strong late in the race. Unless something unexpected happened, either Dale Jr. or Michael Waltrip should win this one.

Because they were teammates, Michael and Junior drafted off each other for the remainder of the race, which gave them enough momentum to keep a comfortable lead. Dale Sr. was doing everything he could to catch the leaders, but his car didn't have enough momentum, and he didn't have a drafting partner for the final few laps. From my vantage point it looked like Dale didn't have the car to catch Junior or Michael. Even so, he wasn't going to give up track position. He was fighting for the win, but he was also protecting his third-place finish.

Sterling Marlin was doing what he needed to do to pass. He had a slightly faster car than Dale and thought he could slip low and get by him for a run at the lead on the frontstretch. Dale was protecting his spot on the track. Sterling tried to maneuver below Dale, and Dale squeezed him down close to the yellow line, and their cars touched.

Dale's car fishtailed for a second, then slid low. For a moment it looked like he might save it, but the car got out of position and Dale slid up the track and toward the wall. This time it was Ken Schrader who had nowhere to go. Taking the high line, Kenny was racing to the checkered flag when Dale's car slid up in front of him. Kenny couldn't get out of the throttle quickly enough, and the nose of his car slammed into the right side of Dale's machine. The two of them continued up until the concrete wall stopped them.

I saw the crash, but I didn't think it looked that bad. It was dramatic because of who was involved and when it occurred in the race, but I assumed that the cars would roll to the infield and the two drivers would climb out, dust themselves off, and jog to Victory Lane.

The race was down to its final second. Michael Waltrip had passed Junior and won by a car length. Michael is one of the funniest drivers in Winston Cup. He can take the most mundane story and tell it in such a way that everybody in the garage is holding his sides. A lot of insiders were happy to see Michael finally break through with a win. As it happened, Michael's big brother, Darrell, was in tears, screaming, "Go, Mikey! Go, Mikey!" When Michael crossed the line, a producer cut the picture to Darrell, tears streaming down his cheeks. Then, Darrell looked at his monitor and saw that the window net of Dale's car was still up. "How about Dale?" Darrell said. "I hope he's okay . . . I just hope Dale's okay. I guess he's all right, isn't he?"

That's when I thought something might be wrong, but it was a fleeting thought. I'd seen Dale climb out of plenty of wrecks that looked worse than this one. It wasn't like he'd hit the wall head-on. The cars had hit at an obtuse angle and slid forward down the frontstretch before rolling into the infield. The front end of Dale's car had taken a pretty good hit, but it didn't look terrible. I thought Dale would hop out and run to Victory Lane to be with his driver. Surely, he was okay.

I turned off the television and walked to the rear of the transporter where Scott Whitmore had pulled the Suburban around to take me across the street to the airport. The race was over. Michael Waltrip had his first victory in 463 Winston Cup starts. I was sure that Dale would be okay.

As I exited the infield, I saw Teresa, Dale's wife, running toward the infield hospital with a worried look on her face. That wasn't unusual. Most wives and girlfriends looked worried after crashes. I figured Dale was probably banged up from the crash. I didn't see the worried looks on the faces of the emergency workers when they arrived at Dale's car. I didn't see the blue tarp go over the car, which only happens when things are really bad. I didn't see Kenny Schrader slide down the infield alongside Dale, then get out of his car and walk over to Dale's window, his face as pale as paper.

I didn't hear or see anything else until I arrived home and turned on my cell phone. I had six messages, an alarmingly high number in such a short time. When I listened to my messages, I couldn't believe it. I turned on the television and watched the news unfold.

Dale was gone. The legend, the Intimidator, the man who had revolutionized the mainstream marketing of racecar drivers, and a man who had been both a friend and a competitor of mine for over eight years, was dead.

I watched the replay of the crash over and over to see if I had missed something. I knew the car had taken a good lick, but no matter how many times I watched it, I kept saying to myself, "There's no way that crash killed him." Like everyone else, I was in shock. It would take days before the magnitude of what had happened would sink in. We had lost a legend on the final lap of the biggest event of our season. It was like the mind couldn't grasp what the eyes and ears were telling you. This wasn't the way the day was supposed to end.

In the days to come, my thoughts turned to the Earnhardt family. I couldn't imagine what they must be going through. Dale Jr. had finished second behind his teammate Michael Waltrip. Both those guys should have been celebrating with their owner. Instead, they were mourning his death. Then I thought about my feelings earlier that day, how I'd kicked the dirt in frustration and anger at being knocked out of the race with only twenty-two laps to go.

It's things like losing Dale that make you think about how precious life is. You can't choose when you come into this world or when you leave it, so you need to live every minute as if it could be your last. The truth of life is, no one is promised tomorrow. And if something like this can happen to Dale Earnhardt, it can happen to any of us.

Sometime in the stillness of that sleepless night after Dale's death, another thought entered my mind, one that was both sad and ironic. Daytona had made history again. Only this time, we all wished we could take it back.

Nine

Four Times a Charm

*R*acing was tough after Dale's death. Dale was one of the people who befriended me when I first came out, who showed me the ropes and taught me a number of invaluable lessons on and off the track in my first years of Winston Cup racing. The thought of him no longer skulking around the garages, sneaking up behind people and grabbing their shoulders, telling a joke with that perfect poker face of his and then breaking into a huge smile—it was impossible to fathom in those first few weeks. At times I would forget; I would walk through the garage and expect to see him in the bay next to me, or at the drivers' meetings. When I would remember, I would think of the times when I'd looked in the rearview mirror in the middle of a race and said to myself, "Oh, man, here comes the black three." Those were some great times. I was going to miss him.

This was where discipline and an ability to compartmentalize were critical. We had another race to run the Sunday after Dale's death, and another the Sunday after that, and another the week after that. It would have been easy to become paralyzed by the tragedy of losing Dale. We had to press on, just as he would have pressed on if it had been any one of us. To do that, I needed to get a handle on my own emotions and lead our team by example.

I wanted to check on Robbie Loomis. It wasn't that Robbie and Dale were close—they were cordial and had a lot of mutual respect for each other, but they weren't buddies—but Robbie had suffered another loss in 2000 when Adam Petty had been killed during testing in New Hampshire. Robbie had been like Adam's older brother. While Robbie was the team manager at

Petty Enterprises, Adam was always underfoot, talking, listening, and learning. There was no question that Adam would follow in the family tradition, or that he would be successful at it. He had all the talent and tools to be one of the best. Then, just as suddenly as his star had risen, he was gone. Robbie had struggled in the weeks following Adam's death. He had left the Pettys to be my crew chief, but they were still like family to him. He did everything he could for Kyle and Richard. It's hard enough losing a friend, someone you were close to, but losing a child or a grandchild is something so horrible it cannot be spoken of. Robbie struggled with his emotions during that time—a time when our season wasn't panning out as successfully as he had hoped—but he is a tough man and he came through it.

When I saw Robbie again, I asked him, "How you holding up?"

"I'm okay," he said. "You know, losing Adam was tough, but I think it prepared me for losing Dale."

I brought the subject up again at our team meeting at Rockingham. "You all know we've got a job to do today," I said to the guys. "But we've got another reason for being here today: to pay tribute to Dale. There's something missing today. I know you feel it. I feel it. But there's also an extra boost of power with us, something that will help us do the best job we can. We all know what Dale would have wanted us to do."

NASCAR could have canceled the Rockingham race, but every driver on the circuit knew that Dale would have thrown a conniption. "Get your butts in those racecars!" he would have shouted, so that's exactly what we did.

With a qualifying time of 23.401 (156.455 miles per hour), we won the thirty-third pole of my career, edging out Steve Park by nine one-hundredths of a second. At the pole ceremony afterward, I put on a black number 3 cap and said, "I want to dedicate this pole to Dale. It's a great way to show how much we're going to miss him."

I gave another tribute on Sunday when I dropped back a spot on the pace lap in order to leave the pole position open for Dale. I'm not sure a lot of people noticed since we had the first crash of the day on the first lap of the race. Dale Jr., who had been through more in a week than anyone could have imagined, hit the wall and brought out the first caution. Just being out there said a lot about Junior's strength and courage. When the media needed a statement, he was there speaking for the family. When it was reported that Sterling Marlin had received death threats from people who blamed him for Dale's death, Junior stepped in and told everyone to cool it. He grieved with his family, helped with the details of funeral and memorial services, did what he could for the family business, and showed up seven days later to race. I give him a lot of credit for the way he handled things that week.

Rain knocked the rest of us out a few laps later. After a couple of rain delays, NASCAR finally postponed the race until Monday morning. When we got back under way the next day, fifty-four laps into the race, I was still in the lead. I held it until Steve Park made a move on lap seventy-three.

We went back and forth like that for most of the morning. Steve would lead twenty or so laps, then I would pass him and lead for a while. The thing that impressed me most about our day was how focused and fast the crew responded to every call I made, and how quickly we got in and out of the pits. At times when we were in second and losing ground, a quick pit stop got us out in the lead.

In the late stages of the race, Steve clearly had the fastest car.

We finished third behind Steve and Bobby Labonte. It was a good finish, and a great way to end the week. Steve drove for Dale Earnhardt Incorporated. During his victory lap, he waved the number 3 cap out the window.

"This was a tough week for everybody, but at the same time we're kind of a family out here, and it was good to get back out here and go racing," I told reporters afterward. "I'm so happy for Steve and DEI. They did a great job and deserved to have a good weekend."

– – – – –

I was also happy with our performance. We didn't win the race, but we proved to a lot of people and to ourselves that the late weeks of 2000 weren't a fluke. The rhythm of our old teams was back. We had different people, different leaders, and a different approach, but the winning attitude was the same as in 1997 and 1998. Now, all we needed were the victories to back it up.

The first of those wins came in Las Vegas, in the race that had been the start of our slide the year before. At first it didn't look as though we were going to do very well. It took a while to get the car where we wanted it. Then we qualified twenty-fourth, an abysmal showing given how well we had run the week before, and throughout most of the off-season. When we'd tested in Vegas during the winter, our times were great, and I felt confident that we would contend. To qualify that poorly was disappointing to say the least.

This was a test. If we let the doubts from the previous year creep back in, we might struggle through much of the year. If we sucked it up and worked the problem, we could overcome this bad start and have a good week.

Brian Whitesell spent Saturday night the way he spends most Saturdays during race season: poring over shock charts, chassis drill sheets, fuel-mileage charts, and setup sheets from previous Las Vegas appearances. With pizza delivered, Brian studied the data with an engineer's eye for detail. Nothing slipped by him. At seven o'clock the next morning, Brian met with Robbie and Ken Howes, where they devised a strategy for the day. Ken was the guru for all the Hendrick Motorsports teams, and when Robbie first came on board, it took him a while to feel Ken out. It also took Brian and Robbie a few weeks to learn to communicate, just as it took Robbie and me a while to understand each other. By the third race of 2001, the prerace meetings with Ken, Brian, and Robbie were smooth and productive. There was little disagreement among them, and when there were some differences of opinion, they worked them out. Nobody let his ego get in the way of putting the best car out on the track. Hopefully, they had made the right calls this week.

I moved up two spots in the first three laps, and up to sixteenth place by lap sixteen. After a caution and a quick pit stop, I moved up to fourteenth. By lap 102 I was twelfth. It went that way throughout most of the afternoon. Every position I gained, our confidence increased. When I took the lead from Sterling Marlin on lap 225, the car was perfect. We had taken two tires in a previous stop, a call that some might have questioned given that most of the leaders were taking four tires.

Robbie made the right call. He was also right when he put a strip of duct tape on the grille to force more air over the hood and create more downforce. We needed more grip without giving up any speed. Two tires and a little tape were the answer. The tires were a risky move, but the tape was even riskier. Covering the grille cuts down on airflow to the engine and can cause overheating. All the downforce in the world isn't much good if you burn up a motor.

The changes worked great. When I went back, the car drove like it was on a rail. By lap 250 I had built a one-second lead over Dale Jarrett and was pulling away. We won by a comfortable margin and slew one more demon that had haunted us.

When I got to Victory Lane, the team was waiting for me with their fists in the air. "We're back!" I shouted as I climbed out of the car.

Later that day, I told reporters, "Winning at this racetrack today, as much as we struggled last year, it means a lot to me. Last year, this race was the most frustrating day we've ever had. Robbie and I were pulling our hair out. We told ourselves we were going to figure this place out, and we did. If we can run this strong at a track like this, then we're off to a good start. We just need to keep doing what we're doing and build on that momentum."

A week later we were involved in the closest Winston Cup finish of my career. After qualifying second in Atlanta, we jumped out front on lap eighteen and led a lot of laps throughout the day. The car that posed the biggest challenge was none other than the Richard Childress GM Goodwrench car, Dale Earnhardt's old car. Richard had put rookie Kevin Harvick in the car, and Kevin was showing everybody that he was going to be a contender for years to come.

We dropped back a couple of times, but worked our way back up late in the race. With seven laps to go, Kevin made a move on race leader Dale Jarrett that would have made the Intimidator proud. Running nose-to-tail, Kevin dove inside. The two of them ran side by side for a full lap until Kevin edged into the lead.

I was running fourth at the time behind Dale and my team-mate Jerry Nadeau. Both Jerry and I took a faster line and got ahead of Dale. I had fresher tires than Jerry, so with two laps to go I passed him and set my sights on regaining the lead.

Kevin took a solid line on the final lap. I wasn't able to get inside him until turn four of the last lap. There was no reason to play it safe. I pointed the nose low and tried to squeeze every ounce of power out of the car. It was a sprint to the finish. I actually leaned forward as we crossed the start-finish line, trying to will our car past Kevin.

Nobody in the stands knew who'd won. At full speed it looked as though we crossed the finish line in a tie. It took a slow-motion instant replay to determine that Kevin had won by six one-thousandths of a second, or about six inches at 180 miles per hour. Once again, it had come down to our car and Dale Earnhardt's car. This time Kevin had a little extra help.

"There was a higher power watching over us today that wanted this outcome," I said immediately after the race. "I'm a racer and I want to win, but there's no team I'd rather finish second to than this one. I'm happy with these results."

Because we led 118 laps (the most of the day), we earned a five-point bonus. That, plus our second-place finish, pushed us into the points lead, a spot we hadn't occupied for almost two years, and one that a lot of guys on my team had never seen.

It was a great view.

– – – – –

The key to winning Winston Cup championships is consistency. The season is nine months long. You're going to get on some good runs, and you're going to have some struggles. If there was a concern in moving into the points lead the fourth week of the season, it was that we would become complacent, or cocky. It was a good problem, one I would have loved at any point in 2000. My job was to keep us focused. When we won, I tried not to get overly excited, and when we lost, I didn't get too down. If I wanted the team to remain consistent, they needed to see me remaining levelheaded.

At a first prerace press conference as the new points leader, I told reporters, "As soon as you have the kind of success this team had several years ago, you know it's only a matter of time before you have a bad year. That's when people start saying 'What's wrong?' or start pointing fingers. They think if you're not winning ten races, there's a problem. I think that has done more for this team than anything. It made us what we are today. Last year, when we had our down year, it was either going to tear us apart or bring us together. Fortunately for us, it brought us closer together."

I was asked if "making a statement" was important this early in the year, a question I expected. It was a concept I wanted to dispel. "I don't know about a statement," I said. "We just want to be competitive. You look at the momentum we carried from the end of last year, and the competitiveness and consistency of this team; luckily we were able to carry that into the off-season and into the early stages of this year."

The day after I said that, we started on the pole, broke a cylinder head, and finished fortieth at Darlington. Just like that we fell from first to fourth in the points.

I could have gotten angry or down; could have said something silly like "Our engine department let us down," but not only did I not believe that, saying it would have been like lobbing a grenade into our garage. We'd worked for a year and a half to build a cohesive team. I wasn't about to tear that down because of one bad week.

We had brought on a few new guys in 2001. Joe Berardi, an experienced mechanical engineer from Yonkers, New York, joined us in the off-season and immediately had an impact. Sometimes bringing in someone who is not only from outside your team, but outside your sport, makes everybody look at things differently. It's easy to become insular, especially when most of the people inside Winston Cup garages have been in the sport their entire lives. Someone from the outside sees things differently and brings in a different way of thinking. Joe did that, but he also fit in perfectly with us. He had a master's degree in engineering and had worked as a manager for an acoustical design company as well as doing some things with Boeing, Honda, and General Electric. He came to racing after deciding that there was more to life than chasing a paycheck. "I decided you might as well do what you love, and that was racing," he said.

Caleb Hurd, another engineer and catch can man we hired for the 2001 season, brought an infectious optimism to the shop. He had played football at Virginia Tech alongside Michael Vick, so he was accustomed to winning. When he came on board, he brought that winning attitude with him.

Over the next seven weeks, we had four top-five finishes, and we won another pole, which moved us into second place in the points race behind Dale Jarrett. It was a good showing, a nice performance, but I knew we were capable of better. I stayed positive and upbeat, but I also let the guys know that we needed to get on another good run and get our lead back.

The next week, we started a move that would propel us to our fourth championship.

— — — — —

On June 4 of 2000, Robbie told me that he was walking back to the transporter at Dover Downs International Speedway in Delaware when a fan yelled, "Loomis, you're ruining Jeff's career! You suck!" Robbie kept his head down and kept walking, but the comment stung. He had been hearing similar snips for several weeks, and it was hard for him to deflect all the negativity. I did my best to keep him pumped up, but he also did some deep soul-searching. Later Robbie would admit that Dover in 2000 was one of the worst weeks of his career.

We eliminated some of those bad memories when we started second at Dover in the 2001 spring race. In happy hour, we had one of the fastest cars as well.

Then, when the green flag fell on Sunday, we had one of the best racecars Robbie had ever put under me. We dominated, leading 381 of 400 laps. At times our lead stretched to three-quarters of a track length. Afterward I made a point of telling the world why I thought we'd won so decisively: "We had such a great car, it wanted to stay out front. That's the best car I've ever had here. I can't say enough for this team. They did a phenomenal job. Hopefully this is a sign of some great things to come."

It was certainly a sign that our old struggles, the ones that had had fans shouting obscenities at Robbie and doubting me, were a thing of the past.

The win at Dover got us on another great roll. We won the pole and the race the following week in Michigan to take back the top spot in the points. It was also another milestone—my first back-to-back wins since early October of 1999. All of a sudden we were again the team to beat, but the competition was still pretty intense.

One of the things that kept us focused throughout the 2001 season was how close the points race remained late in the year. After we won the pole and finished third in New Hampshire in late July, we found ourselves tied for the points lead with Dale Jarrett, who had won the New Hampshire race. It was Dale's fourth win of the year to go with three poles, an impressive first half to be sure. Still, given the number of variables and differing ways to earn points in the Winston Cup system, the odds of two guys being tied with 2,695 points that late in the year defied belief. But it kept us focused. As good as Dale's team was performing, we knew that any slipup could cost us the championship. That was a great motivator, especially for our new guys, who knew that Dale's pit crew had once worn their uniforms.

One week after finishing third in New England and scratching our heads over the improbability of being tied for the points lead, we led 122 of 200 laps at Pocono Raceway. We didn't win that week—Bobby Labonte put on a late charge and picked up his first win of the season—but our high finish and that we led the most laps gave us the outright lead for the championship once again.

Fourteen days later, we had widened our margin considerably.

– – – – –

In the eight years NASCAR had been racing in Indianapolis, the Brickyard 400 had become one of our biggest and most prestigious events, second only in stature to the Daytona 500. Winning the inaugural Brickyard was the biggest win of my career; winning it a second time was icing on the big cake that was our 1998 season.

When we arrived for the 2001 event, we were a different team, and I was a different driver. Those first two victories I was the Kid. This time, I turned thirty the day before the race: not old by any stretch, but not the youngest driver in the field by a long shot. I was also in my ninth season of Winson Cup, qualifying me as a seasoned veteran.

Indy was also my home, and even though I'd raced there since my sophomore season, the track was still special for me. Parnelli Jones, Rick Mears, and Mario Andretti had made history there. I've heard that in the old days, when the entire two-and-a-half-mile track was brick, the drivers were called rounders because oval auto racing was a novelty. Joining the drivers who have won at the Indianapolis Motor Speedway is a humbling honor, and one of my proudest accomplishments.

Early in the week of the 2001 race it didn't look like we had much hope of winning a third time at Indy. We qualified twenty-seventh and didn't have many good runs in practice. I worked the car up to nineteenth, but we were slow and pushy, not a good combination. We dropped back to twentieth, then twenty-second. By lap seventy-five we were stuck in twenty-fourth, and I was frustrated. The frustration came through over the radio, which, of course, all the other teams were monitoring. They knew we were junk.

That's when I heard a familiar voice on the radio, one I didn't expect. "Hey, everybody's having trouble," Rick Hendrick said to me. It was unlike Rick to talk to me during a race.

When he did, I sat a little higher in the seat and listened. "Quit complaining about the car. Get in there and drive."

I've never taken scoldings well, but this one had the intended effect. It made me mad. I was determined to drive the wheels off that car.

By lap eighty, thanks to another caution where the leaders pitted and we stayed out, I had moved up to fifth. The car had loosened up and gotten a little freer. By lap 109, I was in the lead.

I led for four laps before we had to take a green-flag stop. The crew did an outstanding job getting us in and out in a fraction over fifteen seconds. By the time the leaders had cycled through their green-flag pit stops, we were in fifth behind Dale Jarrett.

Debris caused another caution at lap 131. Sterling Marlin chose to stay out while everybody else came in. We put on two tires and made a minor chassis adjustment, but the crew did it so quickly we were the first car back out. That put us in second place. On lap 135, I got a good jump on a restart and drove past Sterling pretty easily.

We kept the lead the rest of the afternoon, going from twenty-seventh and junk to being the only three-time Brickyard 400 winners. That was what this team was all about.

"That was something else, Bud," Robbie said as we stood together in Victory Lane.

"I figured if we didn't win, you were going to wring my neck for the way I was talking to you at the beginning," I said.

"You'd be right. I'm just glad I didn't have to take you out."

In our postrace press conference, one of the local reporters said, "Jeff, the last three winners of the Brickyard 400 have gone on to win the Winston Cup championship. Do you like your chances, now?"

"Yesterday, I thought that was a coincidence," I said. "Today, I hope it's true."

A week later we won again at Watkins Glen, our fifth win of the year, and the second time that season we'd won two races back-to-back. If anyone had any questions about the abilities of this team, or Robbie Loomis as a crew chief, they were answered by the end of August. What had been our most abysmal month the year before had been our best in 2001. We won two more poles in the four weeks following our Watkins Glen victory, along with a second-, a third-, and a seventh-place finish. We were on another roll at just the right time. Everything clicked, and our future seemed bright.

Then, like the rest of the world, we were slapped back to reality.

– – – – –

I was home in Florida on September 11, 2001. I slept in that morning. Our previous race had been on Saturday night in Richmond, and I'd compressed my appearance schedule for the shorter week. I was lying in bed that Tuesday morning before making a few calls and getting ready for the New Hampshire 300. I had a couple of sponsor commitments later in the week. It was a big deal anytime we traveled to New England. Racing fans in the region had been starved for Winston Cup racing for so long, they went all out the two times a year we were up there. I would call Jon Edwards about ten and go through the schedule again.

I turned on the television in my bedroom. I guess I heard the urgency in the anchor's voice, because I looked up just in time to see the second plane hit the North Tower. I sat up, stunned, and forgot everything I had been thinking.

Like 100 million other Americans, I stayed glued to my television the rest of the day, and well into the night. My phone rang dozens of times. My friends called to make sure I knew what was going on. Bob Brannan called to see how I was holding up and to tell me that all my events that week had been canceled. My mom called just to talk.

I stayed home for the rest of the week, thinking, watching, listening, and coming to grips with the New World and our role in it. Racing was the last thing on my mind, other than to make a few resolutions. The word hero had been thrown around a little too cavalierly in recent years. I'd been called a hero by some, as had plenty of other athletes. If September 11 did anything, it showed us what the true meaning of *hero* is, and it hammered home, once again, the fragility of life. I'd been reminded of that earlier in the year when we'd lost Dale. Now, everyone was reevaluating the meaning of life.

NASCAR postponed the New Hampshire race until the end of the year. That said, when President Bush asked us to show courage by living our lives, I knew that it was time to get back in the racecar and show the world that our slice of America was not going to stop because of a bunch of terrorists. I was still in shock, but I recognized that we needed to get back to some sense of normalcy. On September 23, we did our part by getting back on the track in Dover.

Dale Earnhardt Jr. won the race in Dover in what was one of the most moving and emotional sporting events I've ever been involved in. Cal Ripken dropped the green flag, which was the only flag in the stands that wasn't red, white, and blue. Of the

140,000 people who attended that day, 139,000 of them brought American flags. When Dale won, he carried a six-foot flag out his window as he made a victory lap. There was a lot of symbolism there since Dale had lost his father earlier in the year. His victory was another in what had become a long list of standout moments on the 2001 Winston Cup circuit.

– – – – –

On the last day of September, we picked up what would turn out to be our last victory of 2001. The win at the inaugural Protection One 400 in Kansas gave us a 222-point lead over Ricky Rudd. It seemed appropriate that we would win in Kansas. Before the race I had a chance to visit with Matt Dahl, the son of Jason Dahl, who had captained United Airlines Flight 93, which had crashed in Pennsylvania. Matt couldn't stay for the race, but before he left, he said, "Go out there and win it for me." I escorted him to Victory Lane and showed him where I hoped to stand after the checkered flag. After we won, I dedicated the win to Matt. "He's a strong and great kid," I said. "We were really happy to have him here with us."

The win in Kansas put us over the top. Four more top tens, including one in Atlanta, sealed our fourth Winston Cup championship.

After taking an extra lap in Atlanta and acknowledging those who were acknowledging me, I couldn't wait to congratulate Robbie, Brian, and the rest of the team. After we left the track, Doug Duchardt, NASCAR group manager for GM racing, said, "It's a great day for Jeff Gordon and Robbie Loomis. After a two-year hiatus, [they] have come back and shown they're true champions. It's exciting to see good things happen to good people."

Afterward, the press asked me to compare myself to Michael Jordan and other athletes who are the best at what they do. I've never done that, and I took the opportunity of the question to make a point: "I'm not one to go out and say, 'I'm the greatest. I want people to respect me and respect my talents, but I'm not like a pitcher standing on the mound where the ball is totally in my hands. No doubt Michael Jordan is the best basketball player in the NBA, but he's not winning right now, because the team is not there. If you ask [Michael] whether he'd rather be a great player or win, I'll bet you he'll say he'd rather be winning. I just want to be a part of the greatest team in NASCAR. I think we showed that this year."

Then Rick Hendrick chimed in: "If you look at this team at the end of 1999, the crew chief left, the pit crew left, the head fabricator left, the chief mechanic left. Only a few guys stayed. Robbie Loomis was man enough to take that challenge and come on board. I thought it would take longer than it has to build a championship team. But things just clicked. Sometimes it's meant to be.

"I don't know how anyone could ever say that Jeff Gordon and Robbie Loomis are not champions."

After our 2001 season, nobody did.

Ten

Evolution

7f you live in America and own a television, or if you've passed by a supermarket checkout aisle and glanced at the tabloids, you probably know that I had a pretty tough year in 2002. We didn't win as many races as we did in 2001, and while we contended for the championship late in the year, a few miscues early in the season put us fourth in the Winston Cup championship. We weren't relegated to the table next to the giant speakers, but we weren't the guests of honor either. I also entered a new era of my career with Rick Hendrick. In 2002, Rick and I co-owned another racing team, the 48 car driven by Jimmie Johnson. The pressures of starting a new team and the responsibilities of being an owner of a car I wasn't driving were a new experience, one I had to learn on the job. But those news items didn't make the cover of the *National Enquirer*. My divorce did.

In 1994, I married Brooke Sealy, the former Miss Winston Cup. In 2002 we separated and began dissolving our marriage. It was tough, often unpleasant, and distracting. But we weren't the first American couple to get a divorce. (Heck, we weren't the first couple in racing to split up.) But we were the first to have our troubles splashed all over the front pages of the tabloids. I heard that the news of our breakup made it into almost every trashy tabloid and magazine in the country, which I guess is a sign of how popular our sport has become, but it was still frustrating.

I was still racing, and Rick and I had a new team we were managing, but nobody wanted to talk about that. Every week I had to field questions about my personal life. Of course, I didn't say much. Anyone who has ever been through a divorce knows that not only do you not want to talk about it, in most cases you can't. Anytime lawyers are working out the details, you can't comment on anything. Not that I wanted to. Brooke and I are human. Neither of us wanted to throw our raw emotions out for the world to see. (These aren't problems most people going through a divorce have to deal with.)

The NASCAR beat reporters, the guys who covered us week in and week out, respected my decision not to comment on my personal life. That didn't stop them from reporting every nugget they could glean on the proceedings, of course.

Throughout the divorce I insisted it wasn't distracting me from my job as a racecar driver. I tried to talk myself into believing that while I was going through it. It wasn't until after the documents were signed and all matters were settled that I realized how wrong I had been. Whether it was the knowledge that I had to spend Monday morning with lawyers, or the thought of digging through a mountain of documents, the whole thing affected me more than I realized. I was still focused, and I think I did a great job of compartmentalizing, especially when I was in the car. But in hindsight the divorce drained me, and it showed up in my 2002 performance.

We made some good runs. We were leading the Daytona 500 until I got a little greedy and tried to block Sterling Marlin on a late restart. If I'd let Sterling go, I would still have had a chance to get by him in the race. I ran Sterling down onto the grass and spun myself out. By trying to keep him behind me, I cost us a chance at winning the race.

I didn't leave Daytona with a lot of concerns. We had run well, even though it was a restrictor-plate race, which made it tough to gauge how we would run at other tracks. When we didn't finish well at Rockingham and Atlanta, my concerns started to rise. The Dodges and Fords were pretty strong, but we didn't have the feel I was looking for. Still, we finished second in Texas and led a lot of laps, which kept us close in the points race.

In every championship year, we had streaks when the car wasn't the best. Those weeks we focused on staying close, making improvements, and hopefully working ourselves into the top ten. If we had to do that for two or three weeks in a row, that was okay, because I knew we would soon be on a track where we had a good history and everything would click. In 2002 we were able to stay close in those off weeks, but when we got to the tracks where I thought we should run well, something unexpected always seemed to happen. At Bristol, a track where we always ran well, we crashed; ditto Martinsville. When we wrecked at Darlington, another track where we'd always run well, I began to worry. We weren't posting terrible finishes, but we couldn't get that huge boost of momentum that always comes with that first win. We weren't finishing fortieth, nothing that would knock us out of the running, but we weren't winning either.

Some of the mistakes were my fault. In addition to not showing enough patience at Daytona, I spun out in the pits in Pocono after leading a fair number of laps in the middle of the race. "Sorry, guys," I said over the radio, because it was all I could say. When you've won some races, you can get away with some mistakes. When you're on a winless streak that is moving into the fourteenth-, fifteenth-, sixteenth-race realm, minor mistakes become major mistakes. Throw in that the divorce had put me under great scrutiny, and I was feeling a lot of pressure.

The media made a huge deal of the winless streak because of my divorce.

Piling insult on top of injury, a rookie driver who shared my shop and occasionally called me "boss" had two wins and was vying for the championship while we continued to search for our way.

— — — —

I'd known Jimmie Johnson for a year, and I liked what I had seen. He was a great driver with a lot of talent; confident, but appropriately humble; articulate and smart without appearing aloof. Jimmie had what it took to be a sponsor's dream. Plenty of Winston Cup owners were chomping at the bit to sign him.

In the summer of 2000 Jimmie and I were racing together in Michigan in the Busch series. After the drivers' meeting Jimmie tapped me on the shoulder. "Can I talk to you for a minute?"

"Sure," I said. "What's up?"

He told me about some Winston Cup opportunities that were coming his way. "I'm excited," he said. "But I want to be smart about it. I don't want to get into a deal that I regret later."

"You're right," I said. "Do me a favor."

"What's that?"

"Don't make any commitments until I get back with you. I might have something you'll really like."

That Monday I went to Rick Hendrick's office and said, "What do you think of Jimmie Johnson?"

Rick said he knew him and liked what he'd seen.

"Well, if you like him, we need to sign him pretty quickly."

Rick and I were building a new shop a hundred yards from

the Hendrick Motorsports corporate office. The idea was to have two cars and two crew chiefs under one roof as one big team. Rick had taken the concept from Formula One and modified it to his own philosophy; he hoped to break down all physical as well as psychological barriers between teams. Our first thought was to put our team and Jerry Nadeau's team under one roof. I was proposing a slight change in plans.

"If we're going to put two teams in that building, we should lock Jimmie up before he goes with one of those other teams," I said.

Rick liked Jimmie and understood where I was coming from. There was only one problem: "We don't have a sponsor, or a car," Rick said.

"I know," I told him. "But as I recall, you took a similar chance on another young driver you believed in. I think we've got an opportunity with Jimmie we can't pass up."

Rick was sold, but he made another point: "You're going to have to do some serious selling. Any sponsor is going to want your endorsement on this deal."

I knew that. What I didn't know at the time was how much time and energy I would spend finding a sponsor for our new team. This was huge step for me. It was then that I got my first taste of what being a team owner was all about. For the first time, I was betting on a driver who wasn't me. It was a sobering several weeks.

When we had our meeting with the top management of Lowe's in Rick's office, I was pitching like I'd never pitched before. At one point during the marathon meeting, I thought, "Man, this is hard work." I found a new respect for people who sell sponsorships for a living. As the meeting stretched two, three, then four hours long, it became evident that we were making progress.

Then Jimmie called me on my cell phone.

"Where are you?" I said.

"I'm driving back from the airport. We just landed. Are you still at the office?"

"Yeah, and so are the guys from Lowe's."

"You're kidding."

"No, you need to get over here."

Jimmie walked into the conference room about twenty minutes later. After the perfunctory introductions and a few softball questions, the chairman of Lowe's asked the question that sealed the deal: "Jimmie, I've just want to know one thing. Can you win?"

Jimmie never flinched. "Of course. I believe I can, but more importantly, Rick Hendrick and Jeff Gordon believe I can. That's a pretty good endorsement."

Shortly after that meeting we signed a deal for a new car and a new sponsor. Jimmie would drive the Lowe's 48 Chevrolet beginning in 2002.

When Jimmie posted six top tens in his first twelve races, we knew that Lowe's was happy with their investment. When he won his first Winston Cup race in his thirteenth start, we looked like geniuses. Three weeks later Jimmie won again. This was unprecedented, and unbelievable. I didn't win my first race until well into my sophomore season and I won the Rookie of the Year title. Jimmie had two wins in his rookie year. Rick was happy, Lowe's was thrilled, and I was breathing a little easier. This car owner thing was a lot of pressure. Having Jimmie perform so well eliminated a lot of worry from my life.

It was a little embarrassing having the rookie driver whose car I co-owned winning two races before I'd sniffed a victory. Our winless streak continued through week twenty, twenty-one, twenty-two, and twenty-three. Throw in that most people were looking back at our last victory in Kansas and saying, "Gosh, that was thirteen months ago," and we were in a full-blown PR crisis. Every week I was getting questions about my divorce that I didn't answer, and questions about our losing streak that I couldn't answer. We weren't that far off. In fact we had gotten progressively better as the year went on. All we needed was one good break to put us over the hump.

That break came in late August at the Bristol Motor Speedway. We won the pole and knew we had one of the best cars in the field. Still, we had to perform. With three laps to go, it looked like we might come up short again. Rusty Wallace had a pretty healthy lead, although we had a faster car. Our break came when Rusty got caught up in lap traffic. I caught him quickly, but Rusty did a good job of blocking.

This was one week where I refused to be blocked. I got the grille of my car on Rusty's rear and nudged him just enough to cause him to wiggle and get out of the throttle. That was all the room I needed. I slid by, which made Rusty furious. Afterward he said, "I tried desperately to knock the hell out of him, but I just couldn't catch him. It's been a long time since I've won. I guess my day's coming, but, man, I tried real hard."

It had been a long time since we'd won, too. When I pulled into Victory Lane, I climbed out of the window and soaked up the celebration. It felt like my first win. I wanted to savor the moment for as long as I could. One thing I'd learned from my past struggles was that you never know when your next win is going to come, so you need to appreciate the moment. I'd also been reminded that we aren't promised tomorrow. You need to live every minute of life to its fullest.

When I got out of the car and greeted the team, Rick Hendrick grabbed me and gave me a huge bear hug. "Great to get this one," Rick said. "Just great."

Then Robbie grabbed me and put an arm around my shoulder. "Good run, Bud. Whew, am I glad to get that monkey off our backs."

"Not as glad as I am," I said. "But I couldn't have done it without you."

Robbie smiled and nodded. "We couldn't have done it without you, either."

Our ongoing argument, one we will probably never resolve.

— — — — —

A lot of people wrote or said that I changed after the 2002 season, as if I somehow became a different person after my divorce. It's not true, but I can see how someone might make that assumption. I'm no social anthropologist, but, from everything I've heard and read, most men go through a transition in their early thirties. Some call it "getting comfortable in your own skin," and others simply refer to as "maturing." I like to think that I'm the same person at thirty-two that I was at twenty-five, only a little older, a little wiser, and hopefully, a little more comfortable with my life.

In my twenties, when I first started experiencing success and all the trappings that go with being a semifamous sports figure, I tried to separate my personal and professional life by isolating myself when I wasn't racing. I moved to Florida to get away from the hoopla of Winston Cup during my downtime, and while I loved my home down there, it was really a symbol of my attempt to remain as normal as possible when I wasn't on the track.

As I've gotten older, I realize that I can be more open without jeopardizing my personal life. That doesn't mean I've changed; it just means I feel comfortable letting more people see the real me.

Like the fan at Watkins Glen who got an unlikely visit the Saturday night before our August 2002 race when two other drivers and I took a little joyride on a golf cart past a couple of thousand campers. It was a spur-of-the-moment, "Hey, let's go have a little fun" thing that I probably wouldn't have done four or five years before. As we were cruising around, we happened upon a converted school bus that was covered with anti–Jeff Gordon slogans that ranged from funny, to funny/gross, to "Man, I don't believe I'd have written that."

I'd never met the guy who owned the bus, still don't know his name, but I thought it was funny that, unlike other infield campers who might root against me, but also had someone they rooted for, this guy didn't seem to pull for anybody; his whole reason for being was to knock me. When our golf cart arrived on the scene, I hopped out and stood next to a huge cardboard collage of doctored photos. Several had my head on the bodies of other people in various stages of indiscretion.

The owner of the bus looked a little stunned when he saw me. He must have been downright shocked when I posed for pictures in front of the poster and autographed the thing before leaving. But I thought it was hilarious. The guy didn't know me, so I thought I would give him something to tell his friends back home.

I also let my hair down—literally—in the off-season, when I hosted *Saturday Night Live*. I wore a mullet wig that night and had a mock fistfight with a Gary Busey look-alike. Those guys had me doing things on live television that I wouldn't normally have done in front of my bathroom mirror.

I probably wouldn't have made the *Saturday Night Live* appearance when I was twenty-five (although the folks at NBC weren't calling back then), and I certainly wouldn't have made my little infield picture run when I was younger. That doesn't mean I'm different; I've just gotten more comfortable showing the world who I really am.

These days, I can't wait to wake up every morning and live the life of a racecar driver. Our sport is exploding in popularity, and we're expanding to new markets every year. In 2003, R.J. Reynolds asked NASCAR to release them from their title sponsorship of the Winston Cup series, and even in a shaky economy when other major sports were shrinking, NASCAR had little trouble signing Nextel as our new title sponsor. Add in that cities like New York want to build tracks for NASCAR races, and that existing tracks like Texas Motor Speedway in Fort Worth and Las Vegas Motor Speedway are looking to add additional races, and it's easy to be optimistic about where our sport is headed.

Some say we're losing some of NASCAR's Southern heritage, but I'm a firm believer that we have to seize the moment and expand to new markets while the opportunity is there. NASCAR has changed dramatically since I was a rookie in 1993; in 2013 it will look nothing like it does today. I'm excited about those changes, and I look forward to being a part of them.

I also look forward to competing week in and week out. A

few folks have said that if I did anything for the sport of stock-car racing, it was that I showed a lot of up-and-coming guys that you can make it in NASCAR at a young age. I don't know if that's true, and I'll leave such speculation to others. All I know is that I'm no longer the "wonderboy" of Winston Cup. A lot of young guns are on the track today, and while I'm not the old man of the crowd, I have to work a lot harder to stay competitive with all the new, young drivers.

I love that part of the sport, too. If my experience has shown me anything, it's that good people can rise to meet any challenge. Our team proved that in 2001, and we're proving it again every weekend we compete. I guess the only thing about me that's changed over the years is that I've become a little more philosophical with age. Now, I believe that life is a very long race, one with a lot of good runs, and a few bad ones.

The team and I are ready for the next challenge.

Glossary

aero package—the configuration of the chassis, shocks, springs, spoiler, and tires that provides optimum aerodynamics for the racecar.

aerodynamics—airflow over and under the body of the car as well as through the grill, and the vacuum of turbulent air formed behind the car at high speeds.

air dam—a vertical extension of the front bumper that channels air around and over the car and cuts down on the airflow beneath the car.

air pressure (also *tire pressure*)—the amount of air (measured in pounds per cubic inch) in a tire; a critical component in the setup of a racecar.

backstretch—the straightaway opposite the start-finish line located between turns two and three.

backup car—the car that is held in reserve each week in case something happens in practice to the primary car.

banking—a track's angle, measured from zero degrees for a completely flat surface to thirty-six degrees for the most severe banking in the turns of some superspeedways.

banquet—racing vernacular for the NASCAR awards gala held every December in New York City, historically at the Waldorf-Astoria.

behind the wall—the area of a track along pit road that is located on the infield side of the small concrete wall adjacent to the pit boxes.

black flag—a flag waved at a specific car, either for a penalty or a mechanical problem, indicating that the driver must exit the track.

blocking—a defensive racing maneuver drivers use to keep competing cars behind them.

Busch series—a NASCAR series, separate from but similar to the Winston (or Nextel) Cup series with slightly lighter cars with slightly less horsepower. Busch races are usually held the day before the Winston Cup races, although they are occasionally held as stand-alone events.

camber—the tilt of a tire from vertical, a setup variable in racing that is critical for tire wear and grip.

car—a racing reference to any automobile being driven under a particular number by a particular driver, as in "the 24 car" or "the Lowe's 48 car driven by Jimmie Johnson."

car chief—a managerial position on a race team. The car chief works closely with the crew chief on car setups and changes, but has little, if any, personnel responsibility.

carburetor—the area of the engine where the fuel and the air mix before flowing into the pistons; a rarity on street cars today, but an engine component still used in NASCAR racing.

catch can man—a member of the over-the-wall crew who holds a special container to collect fuel overflow during pit stops.

caution—a track condition, signaled by a yellow flag and/or light, that indicates trouble somewhere on the track. Drivers must slow down and follow a pace car during cautions.

chassis—the car frame.

checkered flag—the flag indicating that the winning car has crossed the finish line.

cold pass—an infield and garage pass that allows the holder access to the garage area prior to and after, but not during, a race.

Competition Performance Index (CPI)—a NASCAR formula for evaluating driver performance, which includes average finish, number of wins, driver attendance, and average number of cars in the field with weighted values assigned to each variable.

crew—vernacular for those members of a race team who touch the car, either in the shop or at the track during a race weekend.

crew chief—the day-to-day manager of the race team, who oversees the mechanics and the crew and is responsible for the setup of the car and any changes that are made to the car during a race weekend. The crew chief is the driver's primary contact, the person to whom the driver must relay all information about how the car is handling and feeling.

Daytona—racing shorthand for the Daytona International Speedway, home of the Daytona 500.

downforce—the downward pressure on the car created by air passing over the surface of the chassis and causing the car to grip the surface of the track.

drafting—a driving maneuver where one or more cars line up single file behind a lead car, thus lengthening the airflow over the line of cars and cutting down on drag. Drafting produces faster speeds during restrictor-plate races, where horsepower is limited.

drag—the resistance formed by the car passing through the air and creating turbulence around and behind the vehicle.

driver—the team member behind the wheel of the car on race day.

driving on a rail—racing vernacular for a great-handling car that is fast and holding its line perfectly.

engine department—the members of a race team (or multiple race teams in the case of multicar owners) responsible for building the race engines.

engine specialist—one or more members of a race team in charge of preparing the engines at the shop, and fine-tuning the engines at the track.

fabricator—sheet metal specialist who works on the frame of the car to create the body.

five-point seat belt—a racing safety belt where five straps come together and are harnessed in a buckle at the center of the driver's chest.

flagman—an official perched above the racetrack at the start-finish line who signals the status of the track and the race by waving a series of flags—white, green, yellow, red, black, and checkered.

Fontana—racing shorthand for the California Speedway, located in Fontana, California.

frontstretch—the straight section of the racetrack where the start-finish line is located.

fuel cell—the gas tank of a racecar.

garage area—the infield section of any track where the garages are located and the transporters are parked.

gas-and-go—a strategic racing move where a car takes gas only during a pit stop, sometimes called a splash-and-go.

gasman—an over-the-wall member of the crew responsible for filling the fuel cell during pit stops.

groove (also *line*)—the path around the track where cars run the fastest and handle the best. The groove of a track can shift several times during a race as conditions change.

HANS device—Head And Neck Safety device, which fits over a driver's shoulders and attaches to his helmet to prevent whipping action of the neck and head during a collision.

happy hour—the final hour of practice before an event.

hat dance—the post-race ritual where the driver dons many caps with the various sponsor logos on them for photos.

horsepower—a measurement of engine power.

hospitality suites—usually large tents set up in or around racetracks where sponsors and team owners treat guests to food, drink, social interaction, and an occasional driver appearance.

hot laps—timed practice laps.

hot pass—a specially designated pass that allows the holder access to the infield, garage, and pit area before, during, and after the race.

Indy—racing shorthand for the Indianapolis Motor Speedway, home of NASCAR's Brickyard 400.

intermediate tracks—those tracks that are longer than a mile, but not classified as superspeedways.

jackman—over-the-wall crew member responsible for jacking the car off the ground for a tire change during a pit stop.

junk—racing slang for a car that is not running well.

lap—one trip around the track.

lap time—the time it takes for a car to make one lap (measured to the thousandth of a second).

lap traffic—cars that have been lapped by the leaders but that are still running.

lead lap—cars that are within one lap of the leader.

licensed merchandise—officially sanctioned merchandise where the merchant pays a royalty or licensing fee to NASCAR and/or the car owner and/or the driver.

line—see GROOVE.

loose—a condition where the rear end of the car fishtails at some point during a high-speed turn.

Loudon—racing shorthand for the New Hampshire International Speedway in Loudon, New Hampshire.

lugs—the lug nuts that hold tires in place.

midget—an open-wheel, six-hundred-horsepower racecar often raced on dirt tracks.

modern era—the post-1971 period in NASCAR history.

motor coach—motor homes that are the weekend residences for most Winston Cup drivers.

Motor Racing Outreach (MRO)—an organization that provides evangelical outreach ministry and related services to racing personnel and their families.

NASCAR—National Association for Stock Car Auto Racing, the governing body of the Winston Cup, Busch Grand National, and Craftsman Truck racing series.

Nextel Cup—new name and new sponsor for the premier NASCAR racing series formerly known as the Winston Cup series.

nose—front of the car.

"One to go"—the call a driver gets from his spotter or crew chief on the final lap of a race. Also used to inform the driver that the race will be returning to "green" conditions on the next lap.

over the wall—the area on the track side of the concrete demarcation wall separating the pit boxes from the pit stalls in the rest of the infield.

over-the-wall crew—the seven members of the team designated to go into the pit box during a pit stop to work on the car.

paint scheme—the distinct paint of a racecar, including the color, the car number, and prominence of the primary sponsor's logo.

pit box—rectangular painted area along pit road just inside the pit wall where the car stops during pit stops.

pit crew—see OVER-THE-WALL CREW.

pit road—the road connecting the track to the designated pit box area, usually located parallel to the frontstretch.

pit stall—area behind the wall from the pit box where the pit cart, tires, and equipment are kept, and where the pit crew is stationed between pit stops.

pit stop—leaving the racetrack for service in the pit box.

pit wall (also *wall*)—the small concrete wall separating the pit box from the pit stall.

pit window (also *window*)—an estimate of when the car will need to come off the track for a pit stop, usually measured in lap numbers (as in "our pit window is between laps 45 and 51").

points—numerical values assigned by NASCAR for wins, finishes, number of laps run, leading a lap, and leading the most laps. This numeric system determines the year-end champion.

pole—the inside front-row starting position, awarded to the car with the fastest qualifying time.

primary car—the number one car a team plans to qualify and race on any given weekend.

provisional—a backup guarantee in the field given to drivers who fail to qualify, but who have accumulated enough points in the season to earn a reserve spot in the race.

quarter midget—small, open-wheel racecar, one-quarter the size of a full midget, designed for young drivers.

race suit—the fireproof suit worn by drivers anytime they are in the car.

red flag—the flag that tells all drivers to stop their cars immediately, often brought out for serious accidents and inclement weather.

restart—the first green-flag lap after a caution, a critical strategic period for a team as most of the cars are close together and positions can be gained or lost depending on how aggressively the driver attacks the restart.

road courses—nonoval tracks with various turns, configurations, and elevation changes. Sears Point Raceway and Watkins Glen are the only two NASCAR road courses as of 2004.

Rockingham (also *The Rock*)—racing shorthand for the North Carolina Speedway in Rockingham, North Carolina.

roll bars—the strong tubing portion of the car's frame that protects the driver in case of collision or rollover.

roll cage—the protective frame of roll bars surrounding the driver.

roof flaps—metal foils designed to hinge into the air when the car spins sideways or backward, thus acting like a sail to slow the car down and minimize the likelihood of the car's becoming airborne.

Rookie of the Year—the NASCAR award given to the first-year driver with the fifteen best finishes of the year.

rubbing (also *rubbin'*)—incidental contact between cars during a race.

scanners—radios used by fans and other teams to monitor conversations between drivers and crew chiefs.

scrubbing tires—weaving back and forth during caution laps to evenly heat a car's tires.

scuffs—tires that have been used during practice.

setup—the preparation of the car for a race including, but not limited to, the aerodynamics package, chassis position, stiffness of shocks and springs, and air pressure in the tires.

shocks—the hydraulic cylinders attached to the wheels to absorb bumps.

short track—a track less than a mile in length.

show car—an out-of-commission racecar placed on display or used in commercial shoots or sponsor appearances.

springs—the metal coils that are part of the suspension package of a car and help absorb bumps and maintain grip during high-speed turns.

sprint car (also *sprinter*)—a seven-hundred-horsepower, open-wheel racecar, often designed with a large wing over the cockpit.

spoiler—piece of metal that runs along the back of the trunk to improve downforce on the rear of the car.

sponsors—the lifeblood of racing, these are the corporations that pay to have their logos and identities associated with race teams.

spotter—the team member who watches the race from a perch above the track and radios to the driver when and where traffic is located, where to go to avoid an accident, or when the track has gone yellow or is about to go green.

sticky—a car that has too much downforce and cannot get up to speed.

stop-and-go penalty—one of several penalties NASCAR officials assess for rules infractions. Here, the driver must come off the track and park in his pit box for a moment, thus relinquishing his track position.

tach (also *tachometer*)—the cockpit dial that displays the engine's rpm.

team—all the employees and staff of a race organization assigned to a particular car.

team manager—the big-picture manager inside a racing shop, who handles everything from the ordering of parts to the hiring and firing of personnel and the coordination of test dates and times.

tech—racing vernacular for the technical inspections cars must go through before and after every race.

templates—pieces of sheet metal cut to the exact size of each car type and used by NASCAR to insure that all cars conform to the prescribed racing blueprint set out in the rules.

tight (also *pushy*)—when the front tires don't turn well, thus making the car skid up the track during turns; the opposite of a loose car.

tire carrier—an over-the-wall crew member who hands the tires to the tire changer and takes the old tires behind the wall.

tire changer—one of two over-the-wall crew members who change tires.

tire specialist—crew member responsible for measuring wear and monitoring temperatures in the practice tires and qualifying so that he can make air pressure recommendations to the crew chief for the race.

track bar—a rear suspension bar that attaches the frame to the rear axle and keeps the rear tires centered.

transporter—the large truck that houses the primary and backup cars, the pit cart, tools, uniforms, and radios, as well as a small lounge and kitchen. The transporter is the team's central office during race weekend.

tri-oval—a track configured like a triangle with rounded corners.

Victory Lane—a section of the infield designated for the winning car and team.

wheelbase—the distance between the axles.

white flag—the flag that tells drivers that the lead car has one lap to go in the race.

wind tunnel—a testing tool where air is fired over the car from various angles to gauge the car's aerodynamics.

window net—A nylon mesh screen that covers the driver's side window.

Jeff Gordon
Career Highlights

Four-time Winston Cup Champion (1995, 1997, 1998, 2001)

Two-time Daytona 500 Winner (1997, 1999)

Three-time Brickyard 400 Winner (1994, 1998, 2001)

Five-time Southern 500 Winner (1995, 1996, 1997, 1998, 2002)

1997 Winston Million Winner

Four-time Winston No Bull 5 Winner

Three-time Champion of The Winston (1995, 1997, 2001)

Holds a record seven road-course victories

2002—Recorded three wins, including his sixtieth career victory, captured at Darlington Speedway, won three poles, had thirteen top-five finishes, and twenty top tens. Surpassed the $50-million mark in career earnings.

2001—Won the Winston Cup Championship, becoming only the third driver in history to win four championships in his career. Led the series in wins with six, poles with six, top fives with eighteen, top tens with twenty-four, races led with twenty-five, and laps led with a total of 2,032. He also became the first driver in history to eclipse the $10-million mark in single-season earnings.

2000—With three wins, three poles, eleven top fives, and twenty-two top tens, Jeff became the youngest driver in history to reach fifty career wins.

1999—With seven victories, Jeff became the youngest driver in history to win the most races for five consecutive years. He also won seven poles and led the most laps with 1,320, posting eighteen top-five and twenty-one top-ten finishes.

1998—Won the Winston Cup Championship with thirteen victories, seven poles, twenty-six top-five and twenty-eight top-ten finishes. He also became the first driver to win the Brickyard 400 twice, and he won the Winston No Bull 5 twice. Tied two modern-era records with thirteen single-season victories and four wins in a row.

1997—Won the Winston Cup Championship with ten victories, one pole, twenty-two top-five and twenty-three top-ten finishes. He became the youngest driver ever to win the Daytona 500, and the second driver in history to win the Winston Million. He also broke the all-time single-season earnings record with over $4 million in earnings.

1996—Led the Winston Cup series in victories (ten), poles (five), laps led (2,313), and earnings ($2,484,518). Finished second in championship points behind his teammate Terry Labonte.

1995—Won the Winston Cup Championship, becoming the youngest driver in the modern era to win the crown. He did so in only his third full season of Winston Cup racing with seven wins, eight poles, twenty-three top-ten finishes, and 2,610 laps led.

1994—Won the inaugural Brickyard 400 in Indianapolis, and the Coca-Cola 600 at Charlotte Motor Speedway. He also had seven top-five and fourteen top-ten finishes.

1993—Won the Maxx Race Cards Rookie of the Year in the Winston Cup series, becoming the first driver in history to win Rookie of the Year in both the Busch series (1991) and the Winston Cup series. He also became the first rookie in history to win the 125-mile qualifying race during Speedweek at Daytona International Speedway.

1992—Drove his first career Winston Cup race in November at Atlanta Motor Speedway, in what was also Richard Petty's last race as a driver.

Acknowledgments

Even though this is a book about my personal experiences and those of my team, I could never have finished this project without a lot of help and support. A special thanks goes out to all my friends, family, and teammates who shared their recollections and helped fill in the gaps in my memory. Also, thanks to Rick Hendrick, Robbie Loomis, Brian Whitesell, and the Hendrick Motorsports #24 team for their endless patience and enthusiasm as I pulled this book together. Also, thanks to the staff at NASCAR for answering questions and finding answers when I needed them.

More thanks goes to my business manager, Bob Brannan, his assistant, Jeanette Eaves, licensing manager Scott Hammonds, and the employees of Jeff Gordon Inc., along with my PR agent, Jon Edwards, who worked tirelessly for a year on this book. The words are mine, but the effort was theirs. Also, special thanks to Michael Wright and Mark Reiter at IMG for having the foresight to shepherd this book through to completion, and

Acknowledgments

to my co-author, Steve Eubanks, for his patience and persis-
tence in putting my voice onto the page. At Atria Books, I want
to thank Luke Dempsey and Judith Curr for finding value in my
story, and for helping me turn it into the book you now hold.

Finally, I want to thank my mom and dad, John and Carol
Bickford, for giving me the opportunity to live my dream. None
of this could have happened without you.